NAME ______________________

it ■ is ■ on.

it ■ is ■ on.

■ ■ .

■ ■ .

ē	n

c	o

c	

ē	

c	

c	

ē	

c	

ē	

ē	

c	

ē	

c	

ē	

~~o~~ th

n
i
c
th
o
o
t
th
n
o
th
c
t
o
th

o •	• f
c •	• o
ē •	• t
t •	• ē
s •	• c
f •	• s

o _ _ _ _ _

c _ _ _ _ _

t _ _ _ _ _

m _ _ _ _

f _ _ _ _ _

ē _ _ _ _ _

Printed in the United States of America.

NAME ______________________

sit on it.

sit on it.

t f | r th

t
t
r
t

r
r
t
r

t
r
r
t

i ~~t~~ (c)

t c o

i n t

c t c

th t

m

c o

r •	• m
m •	• t
n •	• c
c •	• d
t •	• r
d •	• n

n _ _ _ _ _

t _ _ _ _ _

c _ _ _ _ _

i _ _ _ _ _

th _ _ _ _

r _ _ _ _ _

Printed in the United States of America.

sam ■ is ■ mad.

sam ■ is ■ mad.

■ ■

■ ■

s	i

a	o

s	

a	

s	

s	

a	

s	

a	

a	

s	

a	

a	

s	

n ~~r~~ (n)

r ā r

th

n

n t

r

th c

r n i

t

a ___ ___ ___ ___ ___

m ___ ___ ___ ___ ___

o ___ ___ ___ ___ ___

t ___ ___ ___ ___ ___

s ___ ___ ___ ___ ___

ē ___ ___ ___ ___ ___

c •	• *d*
d •	• f
s •	• ē
o •	• s
ē •	• o
f •	• c

Printed in the United States of America.

NAME ____________________

thē ■ rat ■ āte.

thē ■ rat ■ āte.

■ ■

■ ■

ē	ā

t	th

t	

ē	

t	

t	

ē	

t	

ē	

ē	

t	

ē	

t	

ē	

c

~~n~~	(a)

a o

n ā

a

c

a

n t

ā n

a

n o

a

o

n

c

th

s

ā•	•n
c•	•ā
o•	•c
th•	•m
n•	•o
m•	•th

Printed in the United States of America.

NAME ______________________

this ■ is not ■ mē.

this ■ is

■

ā	ē

n	o

ā	

n	

ā	

n	

n	

ā	

ā	

n	

ā	

n	

n	

ā	

n | ā c

c ā o

th c

ā t ā

c n

o

t ā

c

o •	• ā
ā •	• c
c •	• o
ē •	• n
n •	• th
th •	• ē

ā

a

o

n

s

ē

Printed in the United States of America.

NAME ________________________

this ■ is

a ■ roc~k~.

this ■ is

■

o	c

f	n

f	

o	

o	

f	

f	

f	

o	

o	

o	

o	

f	

f	

~~t~~	(f)

f

c t
t f
n
o th t
f
th c f
t o

ā · · s
o · · m
m · · ā
c · · o
s · · t
t · · c

a _ _ _ _ _
c _ _ _ _ _
o _ _ _ _ _
ā ā ā _
i _ _ _ _ _
ē _ _ _ _ _

NAME ______________________________

this ■ sack is ■ fat.

this ■ sack

■

a	a	a	m	a	a	a	s	a	r
r	c	r	ē	r	m	r	c	r	s
s	m	s	m	s	a	s	d	s	m
t	ē	t	ē	t	r	t	m	t	d

n ~~r~~ (n)

r h

c

n r

th

t o

n

r n

h

o r

h · · c

ā · · th

n · · ā

o · · h

c · · o

th · · n

h _ _ _ _ _

n _ _ _ _ _

ē _ _ _ _ _

d _ _ _ _ _

f _ _ _ _ _

i _ _ _ _ _

Printed in the United States of America.

NAME ______________________

is ■ this

a ■ mitt?

is ■ this

■

c	n	c	a	c	n	c	t	c	f
d	o	ē	o	t	o	d	o	a	o
f	ē	f	c	f	d	f	a	f	ē
i	i	i	s	i	i	i	n	i	i

t

~~n~~ (m)

m

i m n

n i h

m

n t

n th

h m

h •	• ē
t •	• o
o •	• h
th •	• t
ē •	• th
d •	• *d*

h h h

n

ā a a

o

a

c

Printed in the United States of America.

NAME ____________________

thē ▪ man ▪ is not ▪ sad.

thē ▪ man ▪ is

▪ ▪

ē m	c m	ē m	s m	ē m
o s	o a	o t	o s	o d
r d	r t	r d	r a	r c
n f	m f	c f	n f	t f

ā a

t a

ā d ā

n a

ā

c

a o

n

ā c a

fat sad

is thē

thē fat

sad is

n

t

a

h

r

d

Printed in the United States of America.

NAME ______________________

thē ■ man ■ sat

on ■ mē.

thē ■ man ■ sat

■ ■

r	i	r	a	r	s	r	i	r	d
o	n	d	n	o	n	t	n	ā	n
f	a	f	f	f	ē	f	s	f	a
ē	ē	o	ē	ē	ē	m	ē	ē	ē

~~c~~ **o**

o ē i ā o c n c o th c c r ā o

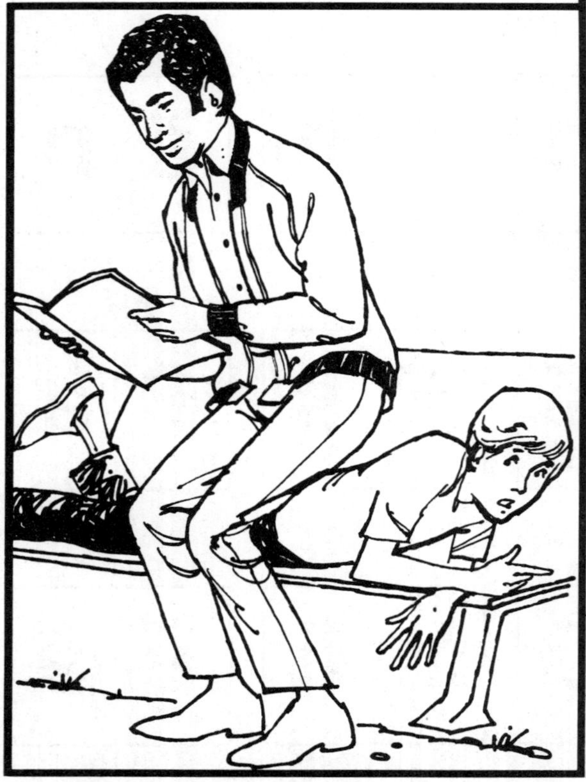

not it

is mē

it is

mē not

h

u

n

c

s

i

Printed in the United States of America.

NAME ____________________

hē ▪ is ▪ sick

and ▪ sad.

hē ▪ is ▪ sick

▪ ▪

a r	a s	a a	a r	a m
d n	d f	d i	d t	d n
c ē	ā ē	s ē	c ē	c ē
o m	r m	o m	s m	i m

~~h~~ (n)

f n t
h
t
o h
n c
n
h ā h
n o

mad	fan
sit	am
fan	sit
am	mē
mē	mad

h
u
n
ā
o
r

Printed in the United States of America.

NAME ______________________

hē ▪ is ▪ in thē ▪ sun.

hē ▪ is ▪ in

▪ ▪

t	f	a	f	d	f	t	f	s	f
i	i	i	i	i	s	i	r	i	i
a	d	a	a	a	d	a	ā	a	d
h	n	ē	n	s	n	t	n	h	n

h ~~u~~ (n)

u m o
u
n
t
u h n
i
n u

c n

sat	mad
man	fin
not	man
mad	sat
fin	not

n _ _ _ _ _

h _ _ _ _ _

u u u . . . . _

ā _ _ _ _ _

m _ _ _

s _ _ _ _ _

Printed in the United States of America.

NAME ____________________

hē ▪ āte

a ▪ fat ▪ nut.

hē ▪ āte

▪

ā	o	ā	o	ā	i	ā	a	ā	o
m	c	n	c	h	c	m	c	a	c
r	s	h	s	r	s	a	s	ē	s
i	h	a	h	n	h	i	h	m	h

c i t

i t d h n i t t o th i h i t

and fat
is hē
hē not
not and
fat is

n
u
h
t
o
c

Printed in the United States of America.

hē ▪ had ▪ a ▪ hut.
hē ▪ had ▪ a ▪ nut
in ▪ his ▪ hut.

hē ▪ had ▪ a ▪ hut.

▪ ▪ ▪ .

▪ ▪ ▪ .

mud	rat
this	mud
that	this
rat	that

u ~~u~~ (h)

g h o u h ā g u h c

g

u

n

h

ā

rock 	**roc**k 	**roc**k 
rat 	**rat** 	**rat** 
man 	**man** 	**man** 
mitt 	**mitt** 	**mitt** 

Printed in the United States of America.

NAME ____________________

thē ■ sun ■ is ■ hot.

a ■ man ■ ran ■ a

fan ■ at ■ us.

thē ■ sun ■ is ■ hot.

■ ■ ■ .

■ ■ ■ .

mād~e~ sic~k~

āt~e~ mad

mad mād~e~

sic~k~ āt~e~

t i

i o t t c h n t i i th

g

o

ā

c

t

sack	
sack	
sack	
sit	
sit	
sit	
sad	
sad	
sad	
hē	
hē	
hē	

Printed in the United States of America.

hē ■ has ■ a ■ rug.
that ■ rug ■ is
in ■ his ■ hut.

---

hē ■ has ■ a ■ rug.

_____ ■ _____ ■ _____ ■ _____.

_____ ■ _____ ■ _____ ■ _____.

---

thē	run
ran	that
run	ran
that	thē

~~g~~ (d)

g t d c d g ā d g o u

g
m
s
h
a

nut		nut		nut	
fat		fat		fat	
sun		sun	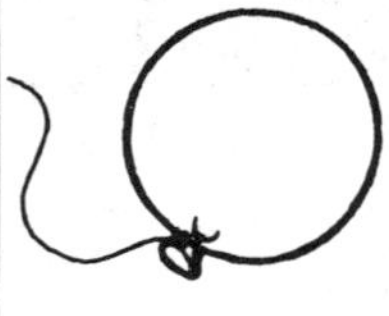	sun	
mad		mad		mad	

Printed in the United States of America.

NAME ______________________

hē ▪ is ▪ an ▪ ant.

hē ▪ has ▪ a ▪ sock

on ▪ his ▪ fēēt.

hē ▪ is ▪ an ▪ ant.

______ ▪ ______ ▪ ______ ▪ ______.

______ ▪ ______ ▪ ______ ▪ ______.

is	it
if	is
it	on
on	if

h n

c h u ā n n h o h g n

l

u

g

n

d

man		**man**		**man**	
sit		**sit**		**sit**	
mitt		**mitt**		**mitt**	
fat		**fat**		**fat**	

Printed in the United States of America.

NAME ______________________

hē ▪ has ▪ an ▪ ant.
that ▪ ant ▪ āte
a ▪ fat ▪ sēēd.

hē ▪ has ▪ an ▪ ant.

▪ ▪ ▪ .

▪ ▪ ▪ .

rug	fat
fit	rug
fan	fit
fat	fan

~~d~~ (g)

g o h d d g ā u g u d

g ___ ___ ___ ___

a ___ ___ ___ ___

l ___ ___ ___ ___

u ___ ___ ___ ___

n ___ ___ ___ ___

sad		sad		sad	
hē		hē		hē	
fan		fan		fan	
rock		rock		rock	

Printed in the United States of America.

NAME ______________________

hē ■ āte ■ a ■ fig.

and ■ hē

is ■ sick.

---

hē ■ āte ■ a ■ fig.

■ ■ ■ .

■ ■ ■ .

---

mēan	sat
mēat	rock
sat	mēat
rock	mēan

g ~~l~~ (ā)

l ā h ā h l o ā l g

l

i

u

a

r

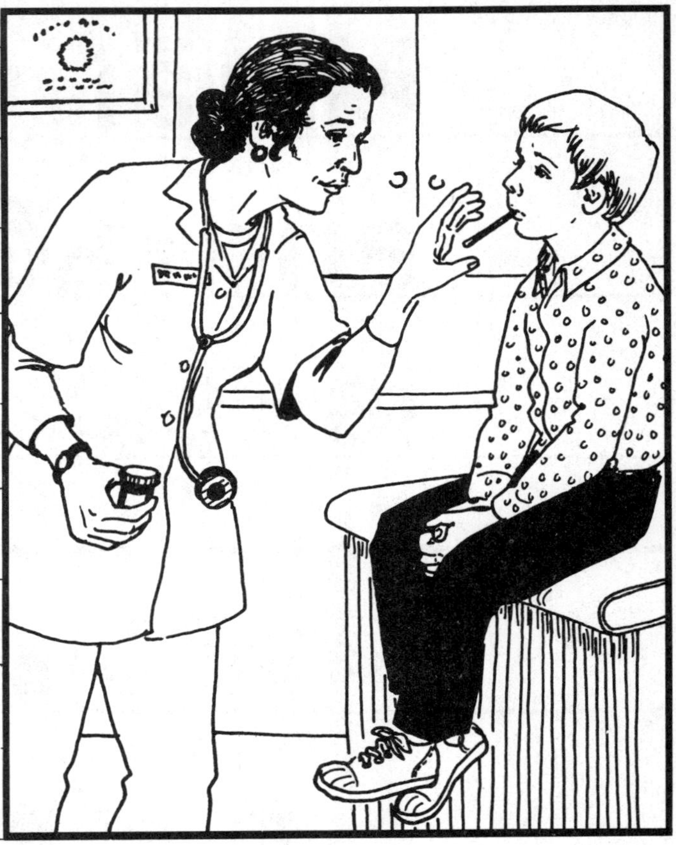

sick 	sick 	sick 
rat 	rat 	rat 
rag 	rag 	rag 
sun 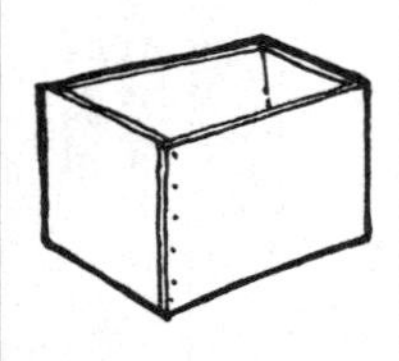	sun 	sun 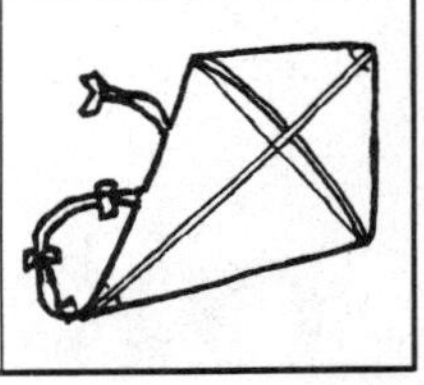

Printed in the United States of America.

NAME ______________________________

hē ■ has ■ a ■ sack.
hē ■ has ■ a ■ fan ■ and
a ■ rat ■ and ■ a ■ rag.

---

hē ■ has ■ a ■ sack.

■ ■ ■ .

■ ■ ■ .

---

hē	sun
sad	mē
mē	sad
sun	hē

o c

c

o l g o

u

o ā

c

c l

i

ē

l

o

m

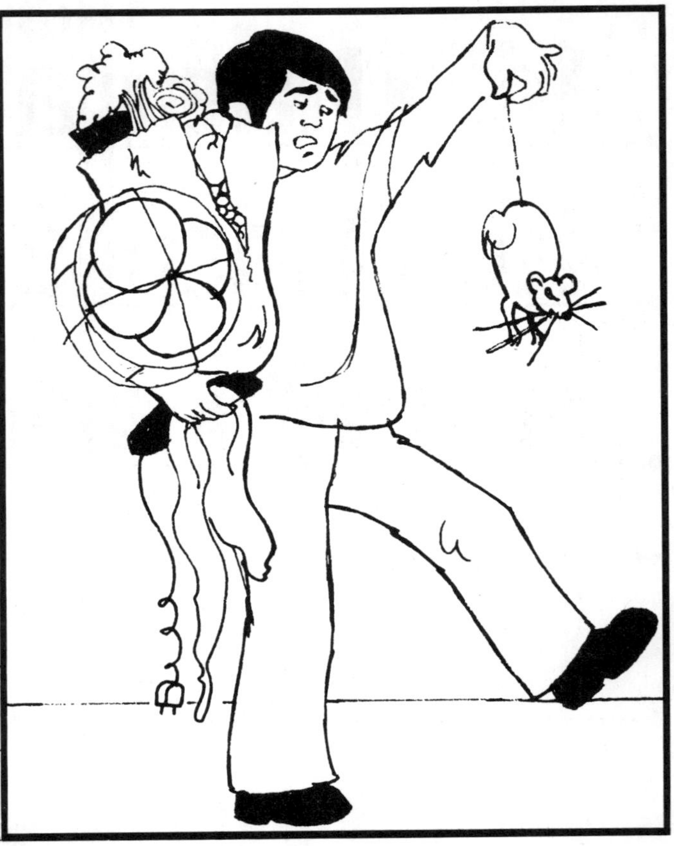

mad 	mad 	mad 
rug 	rug 	rug 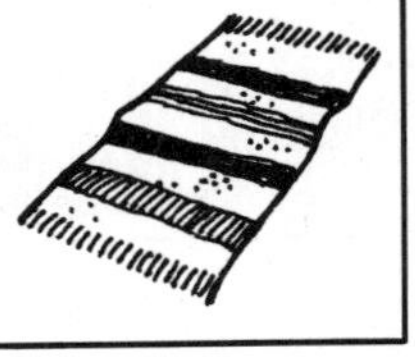
mitt 	mitt 	mitt 
sac$_k$ 	sac$_k$ 	sac$_k$ 

Printed in the United States of America.

NAME ____________________

hē ▪ has ▪ fun.

hē ▪ is ▪ in ▪ thē ▪ rāin

and ▪ thē ▪ mud.

hē ▪ has ▪ fun.

▪ ▪ .

▪ ▪ .

is	has
his	an
has	his
an	is

~~u~~ (n)

h u n ā g n u o c n u

l ____ ____ ____ ____

o ____ ____ ____ ____

i ____ ____ ____ ____

d ____ ____ ____ ____

r ____ ____ ____ ____

fan		**fan**		**fan**	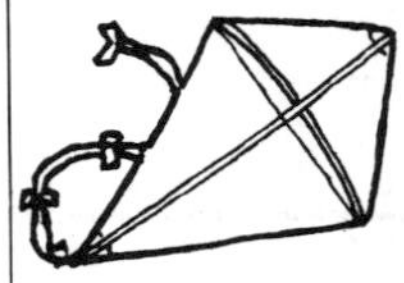
sad		**sad**		**sad**	
sit		**sit**		**sit**	
rag	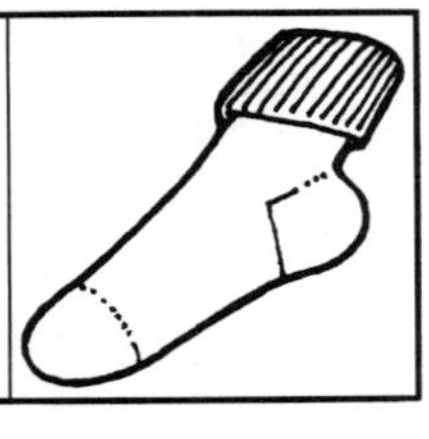	**rag**		**rag**	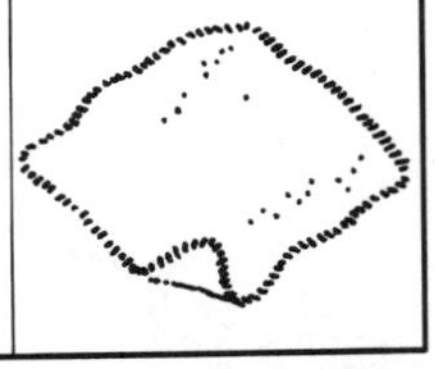

Printed in the United States of America.

NAME ______________________

that ■ man ■ has ■ thē ■ māil.

hē ■ is ■ lāte.

hē ■ has ■ thē ■ māil.

■ ■ ■ .

■ ■ ■ .

fun	sit
fat	fun
sit	sick
fan	fat
sick	fan

i l

i ā l c i g w i l l u

w w

n

l

t

a

mēan		**mēan**		**mēan**	
fat		**fat**		**fat**	
sick		**sick**		**sick**	
rock		**rock**		**rock**	

thē ▪ locₖ ▪ is ▪ on ▪ a ▪ rocₖ.

thē ▪ nut ▪ is ▪ on ▪ thē ▪ locₖ.

it ▪ is ▪ on ▪ a ▪ rock.

____ ▪ ____ ▪ ____ ▪ ____ ▪ ________ .

____ ▪ ____ ▪ ____ ▪ ____ ▪ ________ .

māil	lāte
lāte	sāil
hat	māil
hāte	hat
sāil	hāte

w m

m h w g ā w m l o w m

l

w w

g

h

ā

sack	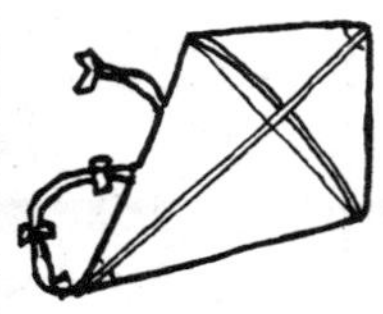	**sack**		**sack**	
fan		**fan**	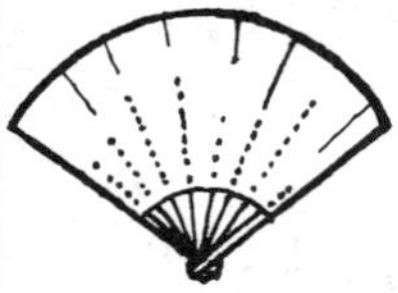	**fan**	
rat		**rat**		**rat**	
rag		**rag**		**rag**	

Printed in the United States of America.

NAME ______________________

wē ▪ sēē ▪ a ▪ hut. ▪ wē ▪ will

run ▪ in ▪ thē ▪ hut.

wē ▪ will ▪ lock ▪ thē ▪ hut.

wē ▪ sēē ▪ a ▪ hut.

_____ ▪ _____ ▪ _____ ▪ _____.

_____ ▪ _____ ▪ _____ ▪ _____.

lock	lick	~~l~~	(i)
sick	sock		
rock	lock		
sock	rock		
lick	sick		

c l w i w i l o l g i

w w ___

g ___ ___ ___ ___

c ___ ___ ___ ___

l ___ ___ ___ ___

o ___ ___ ___ ___

hē 

hē 

hē 

nut 

nut 

nut 

rāin 

rāin 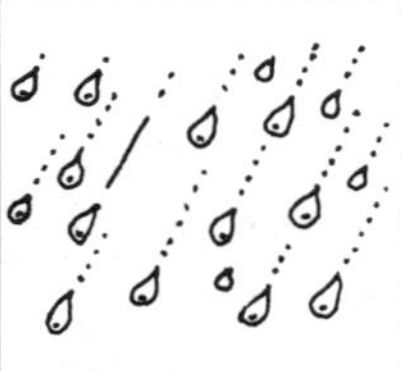

rāin 

fun 

fun 

fun 

Printed in the United States of America.

NAME ______________________

his ▪ nāmₑ ▪ is ▪ ron.

hē ▪ will ▪ run. ▪ and

hē ▪ will ▪ sēē ▪ mē.

---

his ▪ nāme ▪ is ▪ ron.

▪ ▪ ▪ .

▪ ▪ ▪ .

---

hut	hit
hat	hut
nut	not
hit	nut
not	hat

~~th~~ (sh)

th

h

sh

th

ā

w

sh

th

l

u

sh

sh sh

n _ _ _ _

w _ _ _

a _ _ _ _

s _ _ _ _

rug		rug		rug	
sit		sit		sit	
sack		sack		sack	
māil		māil		māil	

Printed in the United States of America.

wē · had · a · ram.

that · ram · ran.

wē · ran · and

hē · ran.

---

wē · had · a · ram.

___ · ___ · ___ · ___.

___ · ___ · ___ · ___.

~~sh~~ (th)

th c sh g l th sh th ā w sh g th sh u

ron	sēē
sēē	rat
run	ron
ran	sit
sit	run
rat	ran

sh sh

w ___ ___ ___

g ___ ___ ___ ___

u ___ ___ ___ ___

a nut

a man

rock

sad

rat

 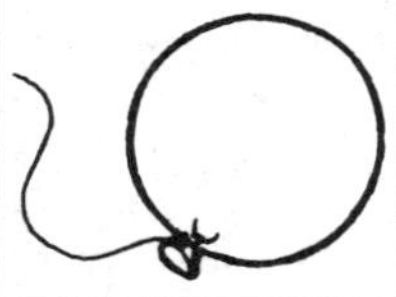

a sack

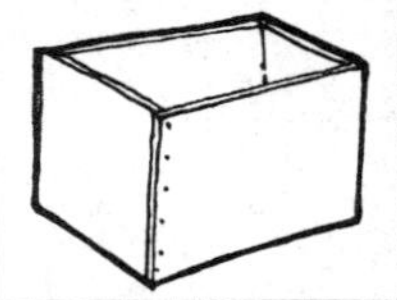

rag

a lock

run

a rug

 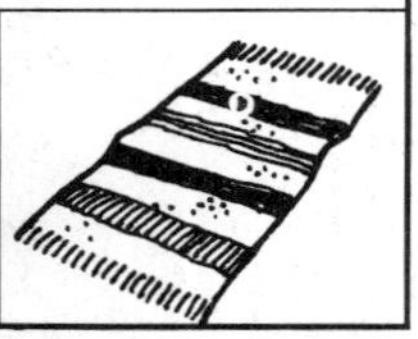

sit

a hat

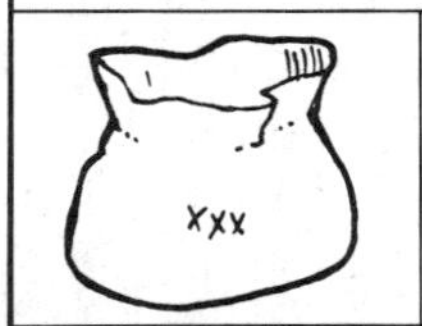

Printed in the United States of America.

this · is · a · cat.

this · cat · has · fat

fēēt. · this · cat · can

run · in · thē · mud.

this · is · a · cat.

_____ · ___ · _ · ____.

_____ · ___ · _ · ____.

n	h

h ā n h h o g n sh n c l n h sh

wē	rāin
mad	mud
will	māde
māde	mad
mud	wē
rāin	will

th

sh sh

w

g

hut

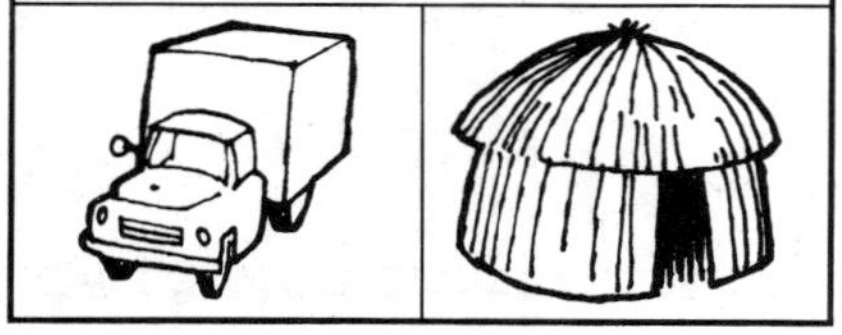

a lock

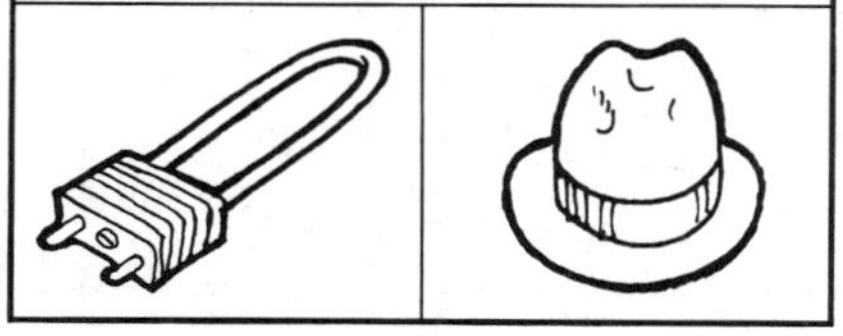

a fan

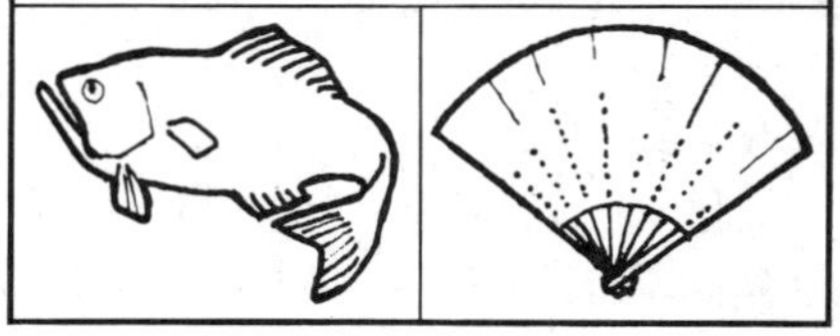

hē

run

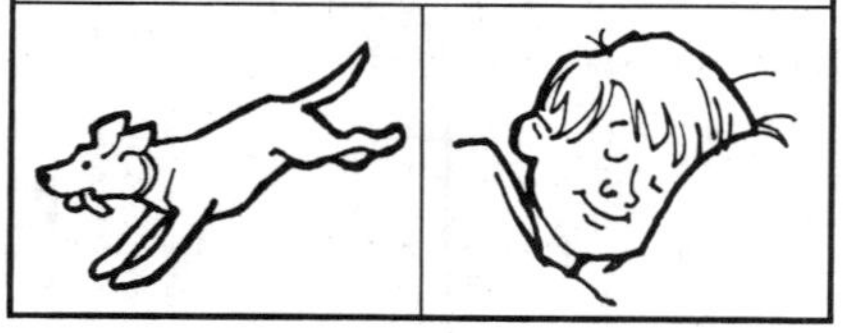

māil

mad

rāin

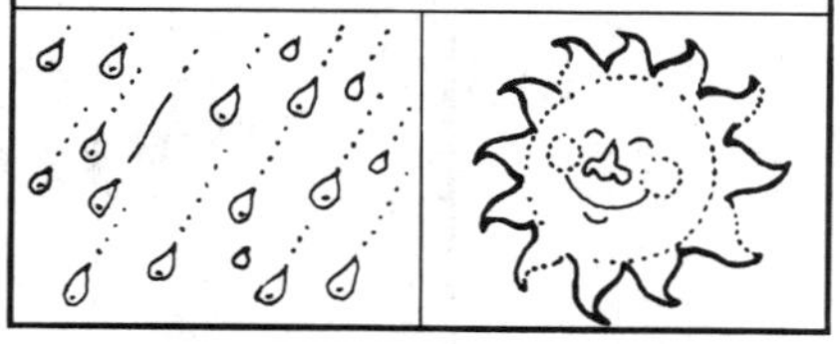

a rock

sick

fat

mitt

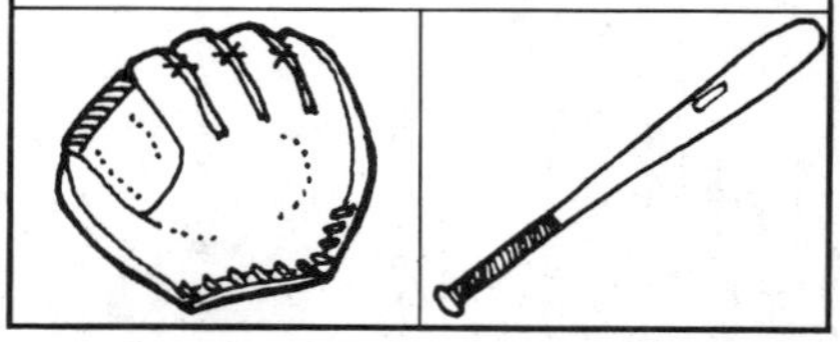

Printed in the United States of America.

shē · has · a · cat.

that · cat · is

not · littl~e~. · that · cat

is · fat.

shē · has · a · cat.

_____ · _____ · _____ · _____.

_____ · _____ · _____ · _____.

~~m~~ (w)

h m w w g l m w m h sh w u ā m

cat	fat
can	fun
fun	fig
fat	fēēt
fēēt	cat
fig	can

th ___ ___ ___

a ___ ___ ___ ___

sh ___ ___

l ___ ___ ___ ___

a sack

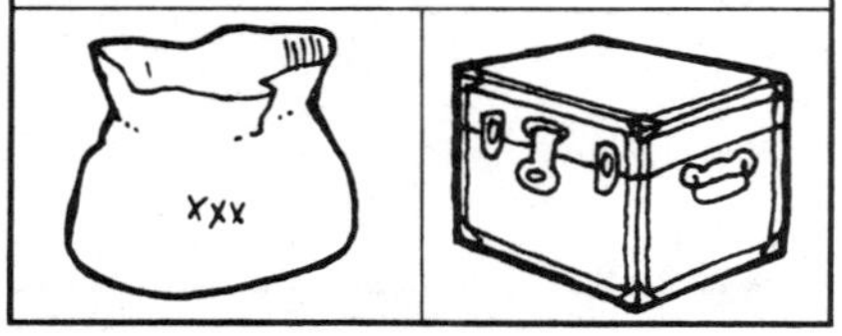

sit

nut

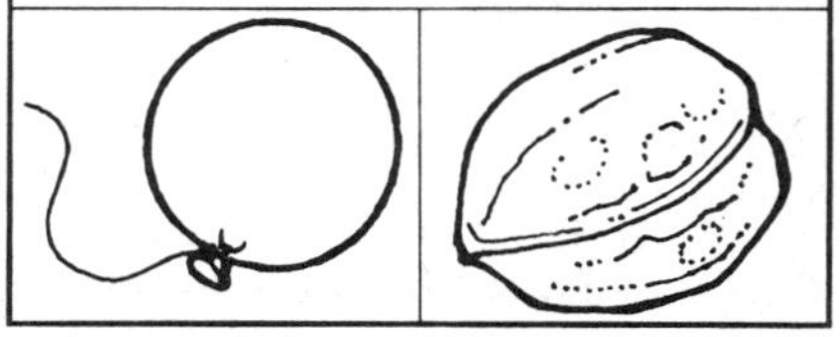

man

a rag

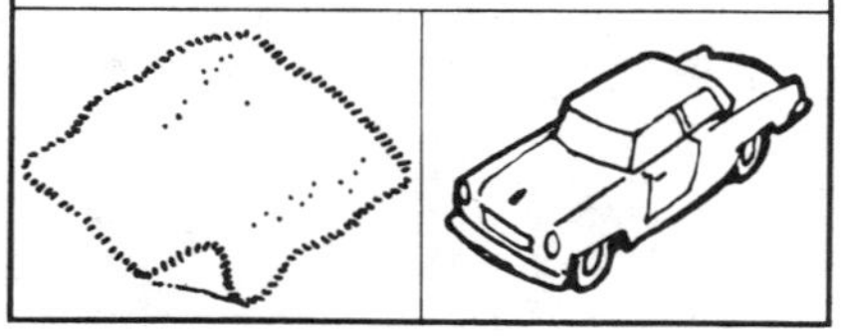

mēan

mud

rāin

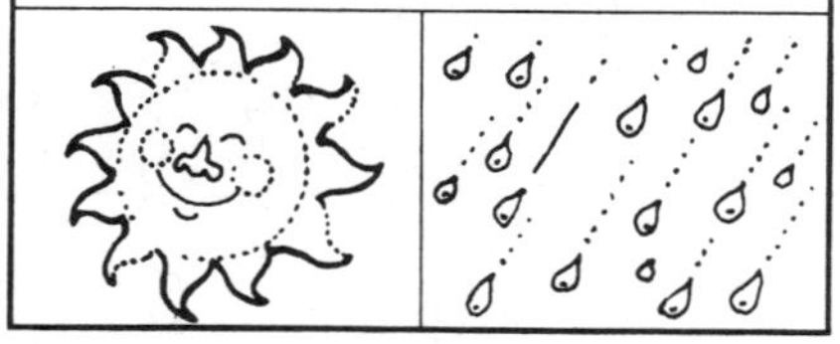

māil

hē

rug

a hut

Printed in the United States of America.

NAME ____________________

hē · has · a · shack.

thē · shack · is · in · thē

sand. · thē · man · is

in · thē · shack.

hē · has · a · shack.

■ ■ ■ .

■ ■ ■ .

~~ā~~ (a)

a

ā

w

ā

g

h

a

c

w

a

ā

ā

a

sh

shē	fan
sat	sit
fat	sack
fan	fat
sack	sat
sit	shē

sh ____ ____

w ____ ____ ____

h ____ ____ ____ ____

g ____ ____ ____ ____

lock

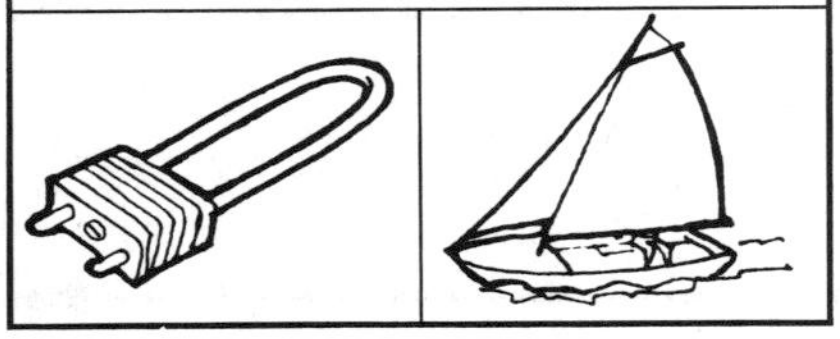

run

mad

a fan

mitt

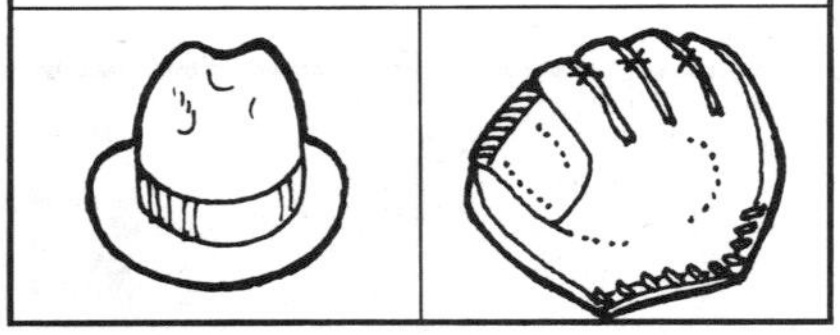

rāin

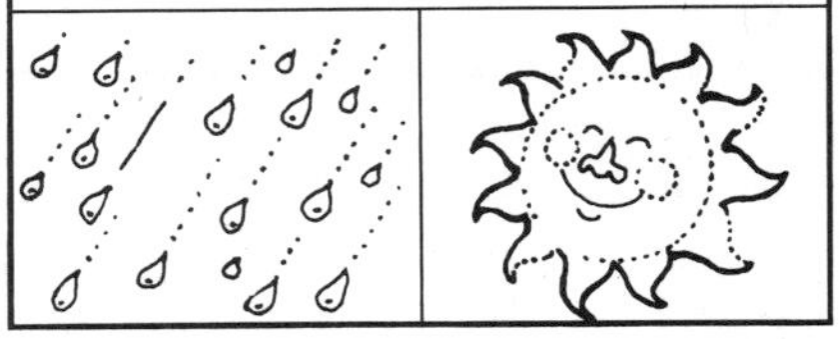

sick

sad

a rock

fat

hē

mēan

Printed in the United States of America.

hē·had·fun.

shē·had·fun·in·thē

sand.·and·thē·cat·had

fun·in·thē·sand.

hē·had·fun.

rat ran ~~rat~~

mē

rat at

rat

wē

sat

rat

rat

rat

rug on

hē	shack
has	hē
sock	shē
shē	sock
is	has
shack	is

o ___ ___ ___ ___

a ___ ___ ___ ___

ā ___ ___ ___ ___

u ___ ___ ___ ___

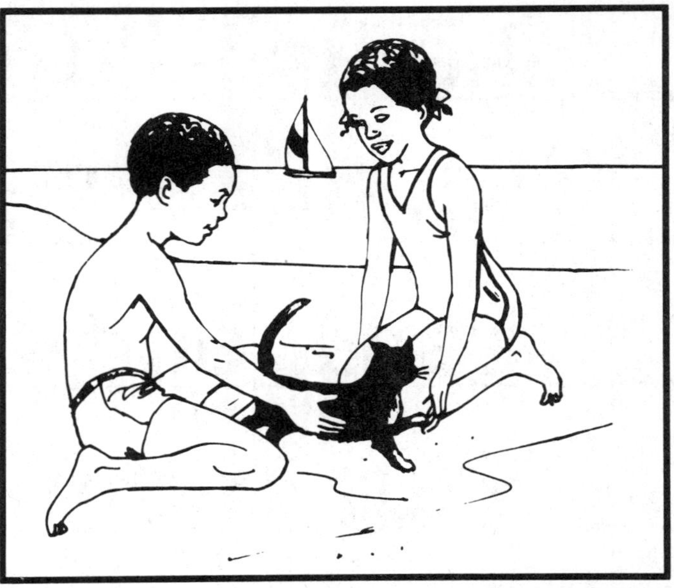

a rat

hut

man

him

sad

a rock

 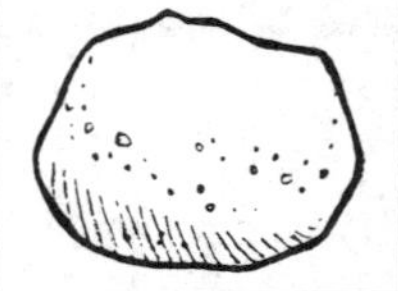

sit

a sack

run

fēēt

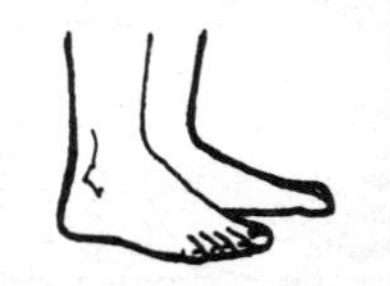 

cat

māil

 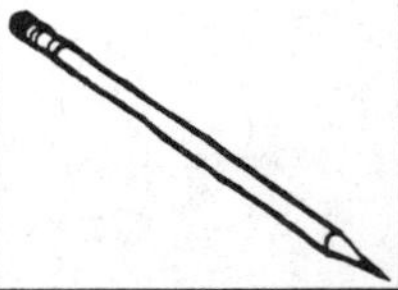

Printed in the United States of America.

NAME ______________________

shē is in thē rāin.
shē has a sack. māil is
in that sack. will shē rēad
thē māil?

shē is in thē rāin.

~~sēē~~	had	has
	and	an
	hand	and
	has	had
	sand	hand
	an	sand

sēē mad fat sēē sēē sack man shē sēē sēē mud sēē sick

i ___ ___ ___ ___

u ___ ___ ___ ___

w ___ ___ ___

g ___ ___ ___ ___

a cat

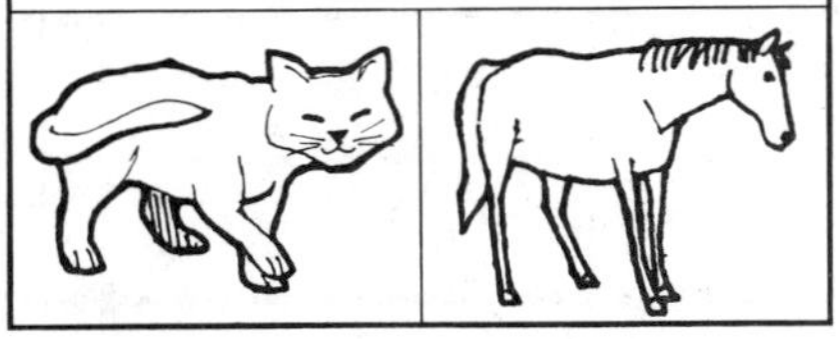

fat

lock

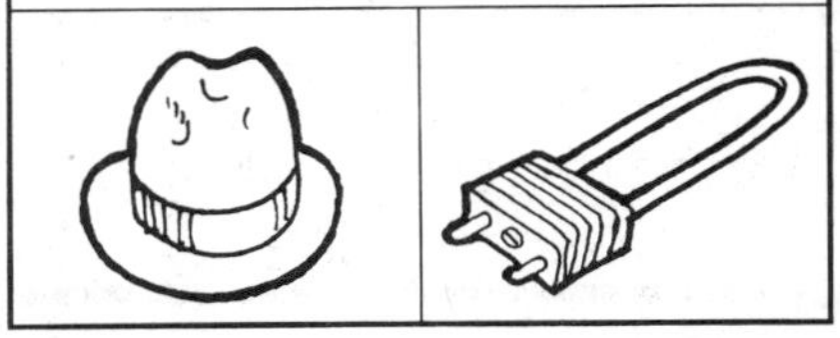

hē

run

a mitt

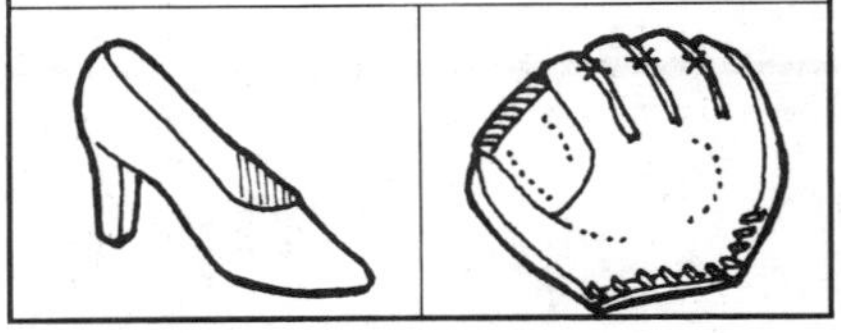

fēēt

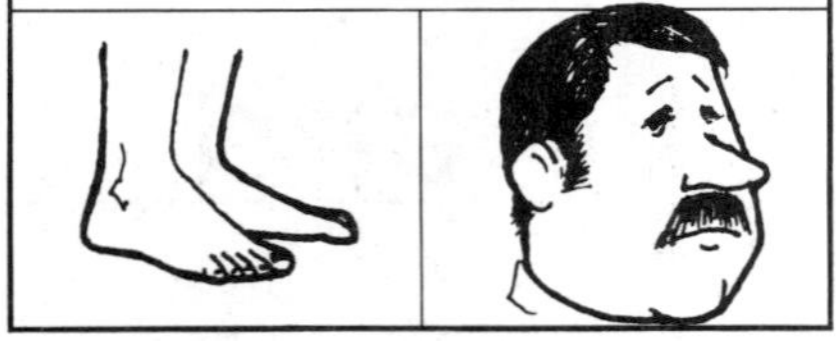

rāin

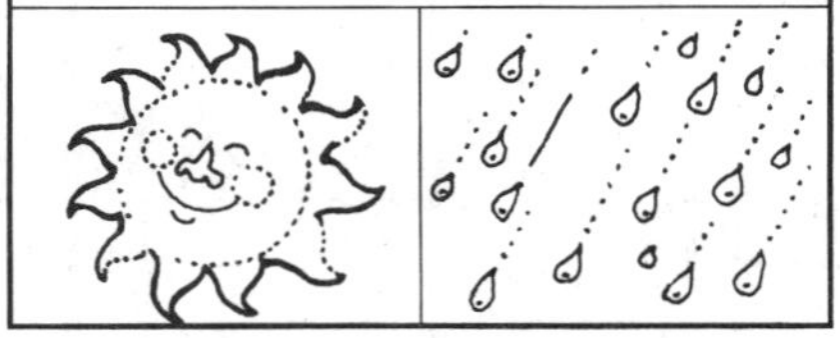

shē

little

sick

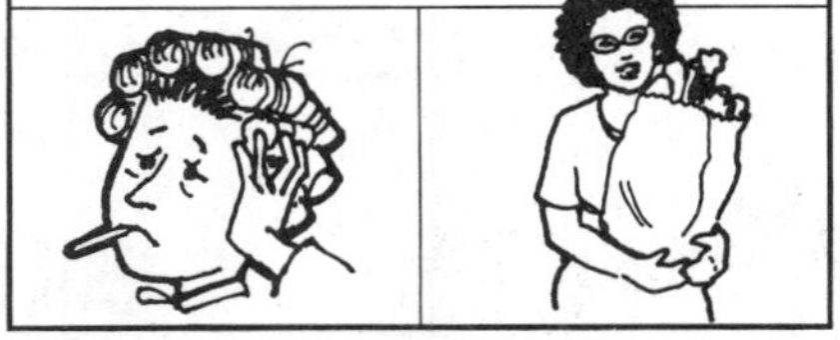

a rug

Printed in the United States of America.

NAME ______________________

sam has ēars.

sam has a tāil.

sam is not a man.

sam is not a cat.

sam has ēars.

run

fēēt

~~run~~

rug

ran

not

run

run

hut

run

cat

run

run

fun

shot	hot
at	hat
rat	shot
hot	an
an	rat
hat	at

sh ___ ___

n ___ ___ ___ ___

l ___ ___ ___ ___

th ___ ___ ___

shack

sand

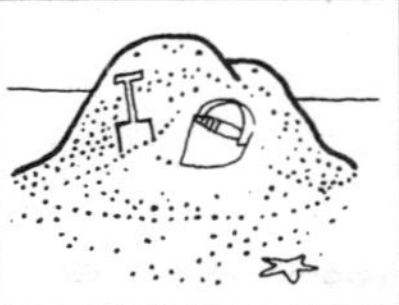 

sad

shē

mud

a rock

him

sit

cat

mēan

māil

a fan

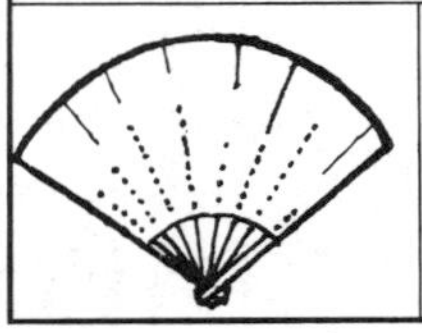 

Printed in the United States of America.

NAME ________________________

thē sand is hot.
his fēēt got
hot. his hat is
not hot.

thē sand is hot.

sat

~~sat~~

fat
sat
sand
rock
sēē
sat
sat
at
sat
hut
sat
hē

ēar	ēat
tāil	cat
fig	ēar
ēat	fig
cat	tāil
nāme	nāme

h _____ _____ _____ _____

n _____ _____ _____ _____

w _____ _____ _____

r _____ _____ _____ _____

sack

fēēt

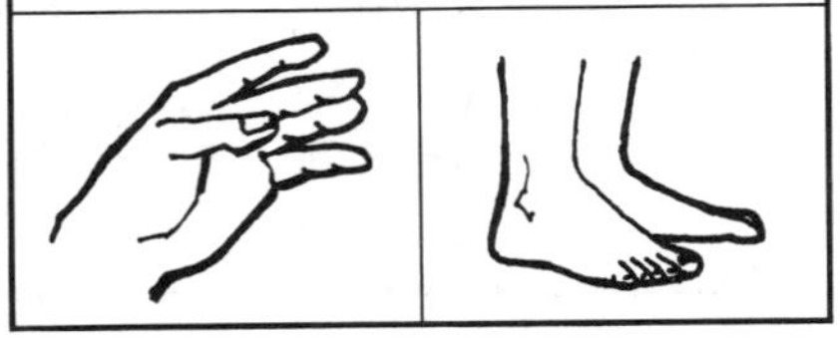

a lock

a rug

shē

fat

shack

rāin

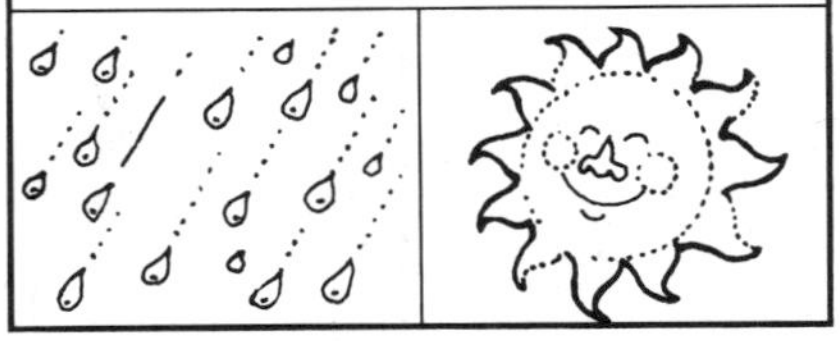

hē

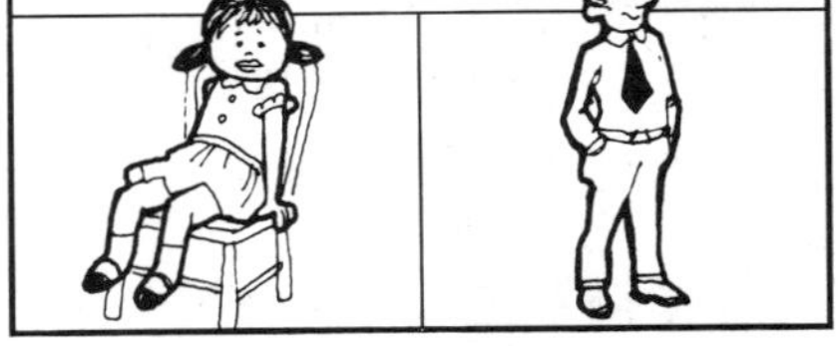

mad

little

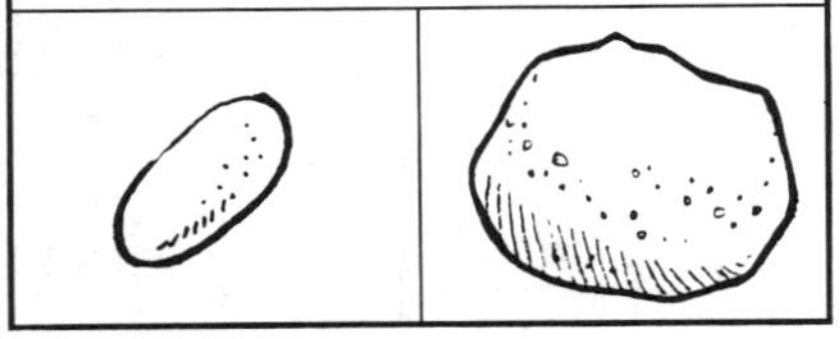

fan

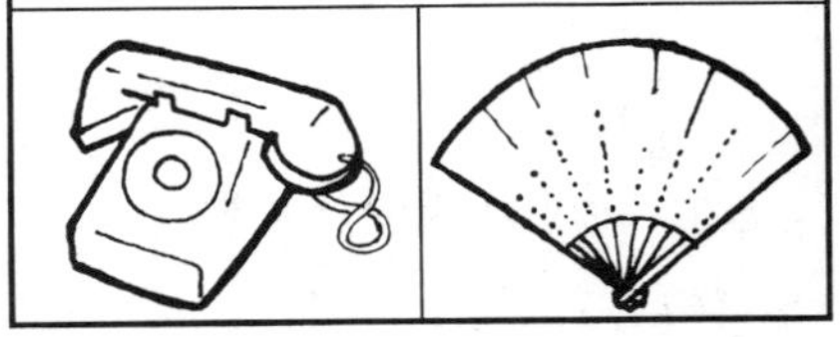

Printed in the United States of America.

NAME ______________________

a fish māde a wish.

"I wish I had fēēt. I wish I had a tāil. I wish I had a hat. I wish I had a dish."

a fish māde a wish.

shē

~~shē~~

hot

shē

shē

not

hē

shē

fun

shē

sack

māde

hat

shē

hot	got
got	not
hat	rat
not	hot
rat	fat
fat	hat

f

a

I

r

rag

 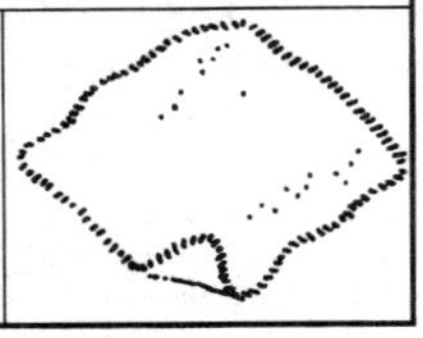

sand

a hut

 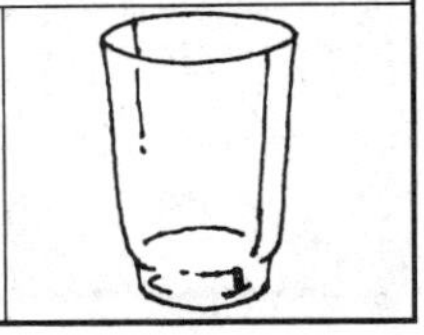

a rat

run

shē

māil

 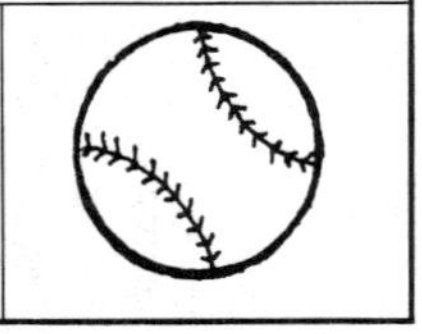

a rug

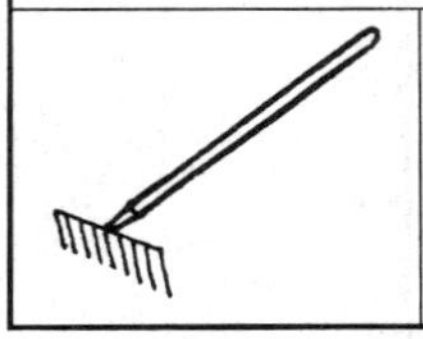 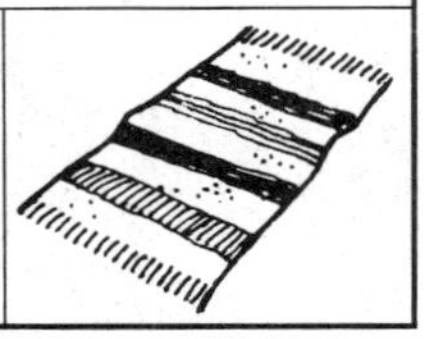

rock

cat

sick

him

Printed in the United States of America.

NAME

now I will run.

now I will run.

I I I	hat
sh	rag
w	hot
l	fat
g	am

~~sit~~

sit hit it sit sit sat loc_k feet sit wish sit not sit hut sit sit mad sit

a nut

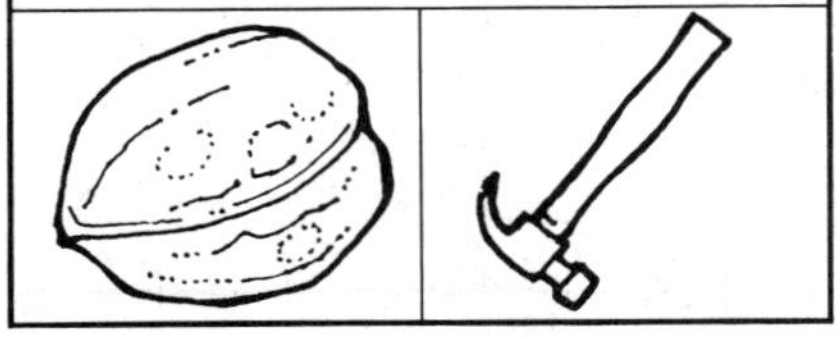

fat

shē

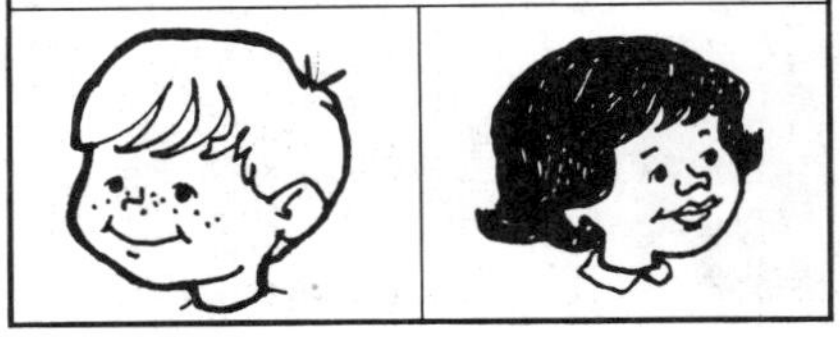

tāil

a man

ēars

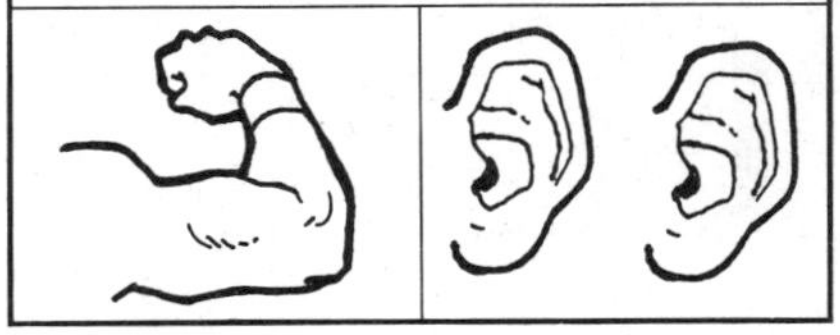

sit

fēēt

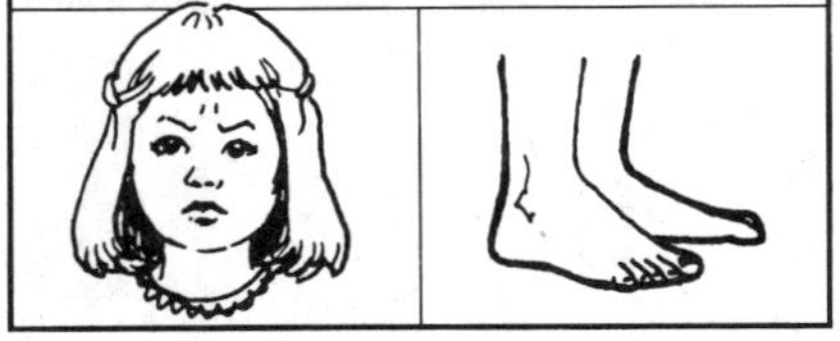

shack

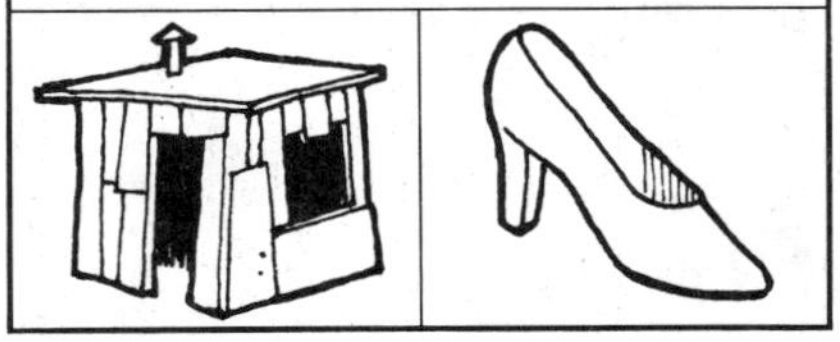

rug

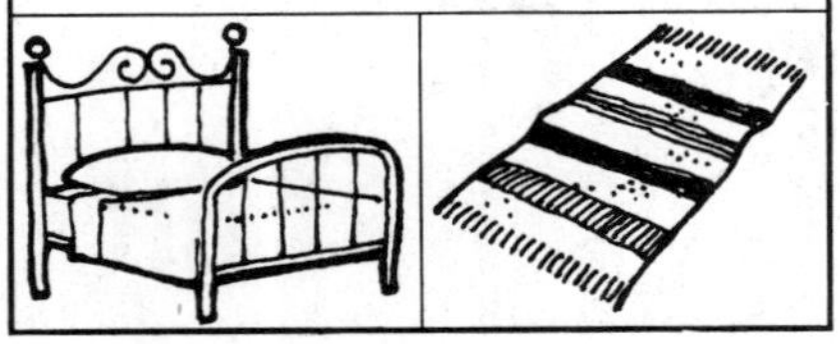

a cat

rāin

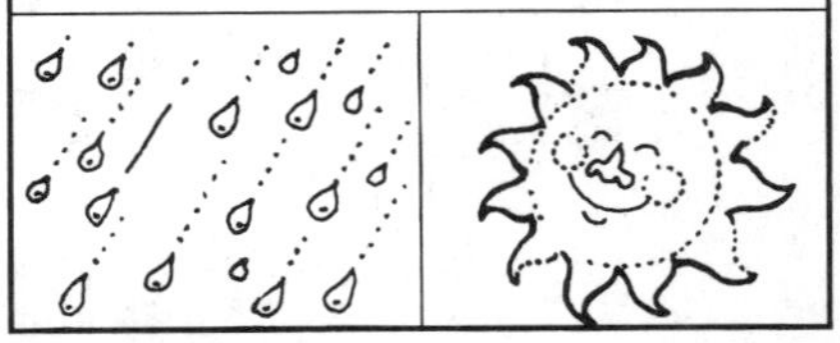

Printed in the United States of America.

I wish I had sand.

I wish I had sand.

sh ___ ___	is
I ___ ___	fēēt
i ___ ___ ___ ___	has
ā ___ ___ ___ ___	will
a ___ ___ ___ ___	sit

~~sack~~

sack shack sad sack rug had sack sack fun sack hot sack sand sack sack late sack ears

a tāil

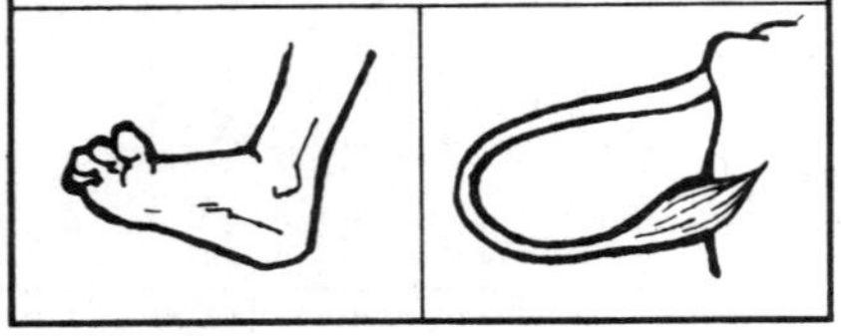

run

rock

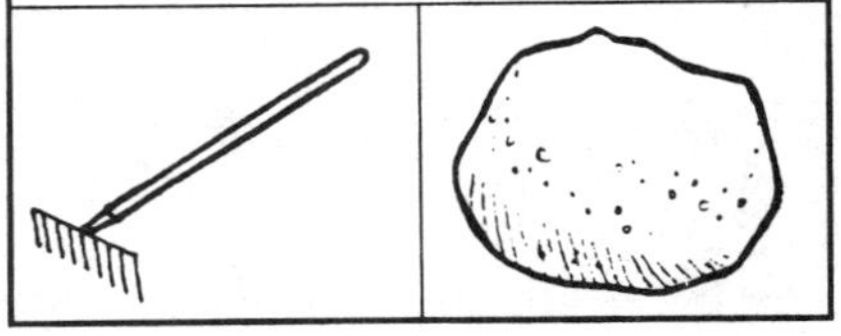

him

sack

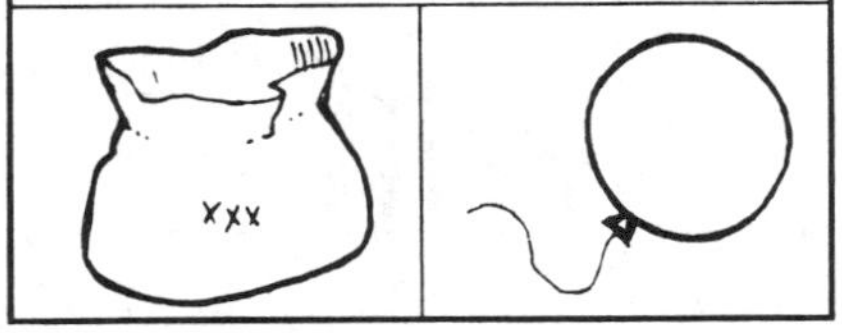

mad

māil

sand

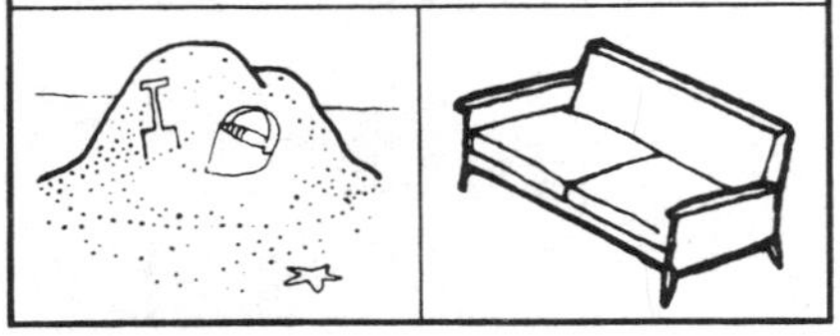

fēēt

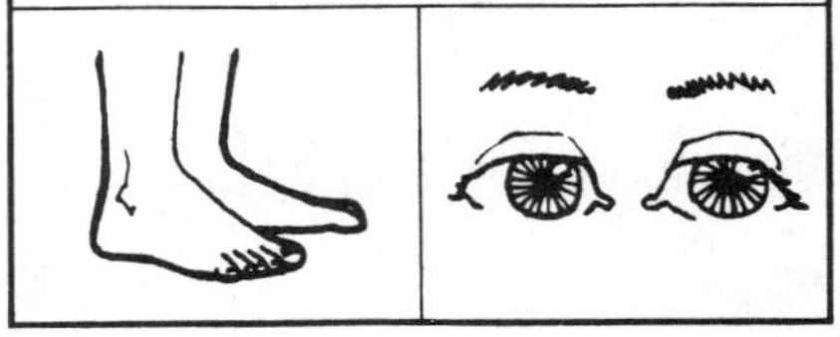

a hat

ēars

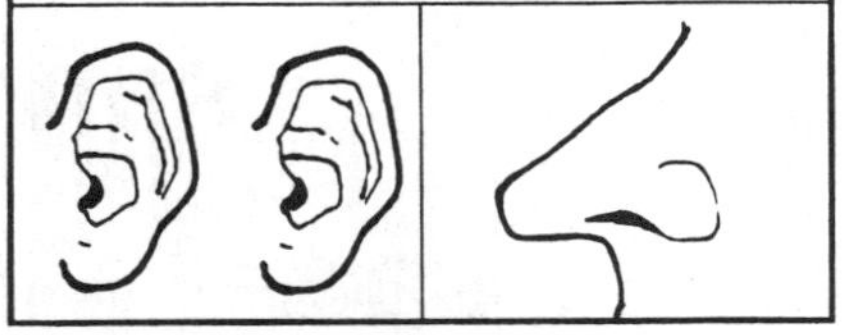

little

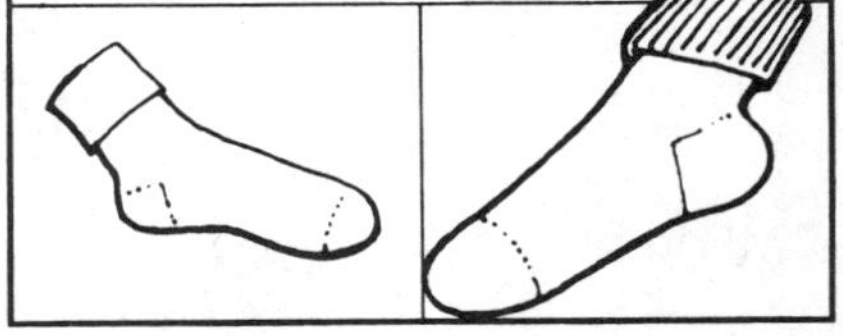

Printed in the United States of America.

NAME ______________________

thē cat has fun.

thē cat has fun.

w ___ ___ ___	fish
c ___ ___ ___ ___	and
o ___ ___ ___ ___	at
sh ___ ___	nāme
ā ___ ___ ___ ___	hē

~~wē~~

and wē wē hē wē tāil run wē nāme got wē now wē wē this wē wē hat

hat

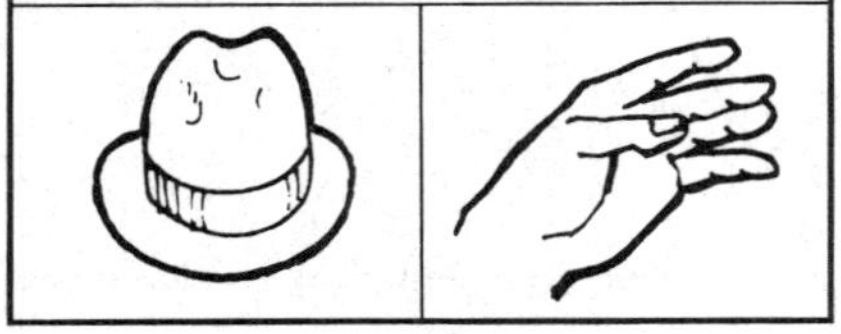

a rat

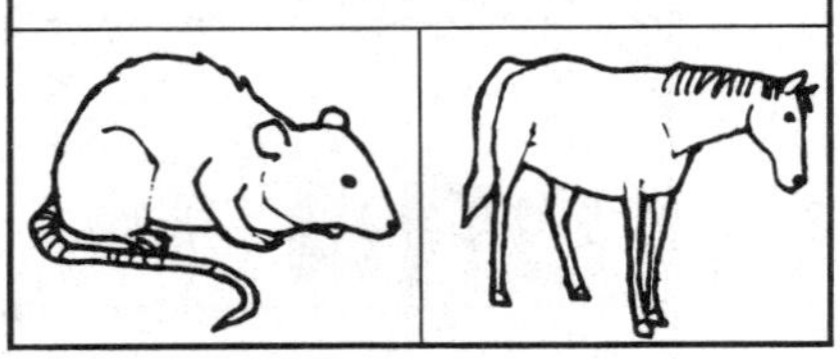

shē

a fish

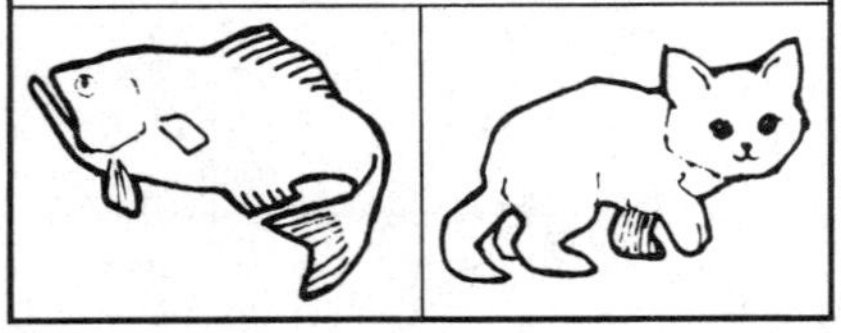

rāin

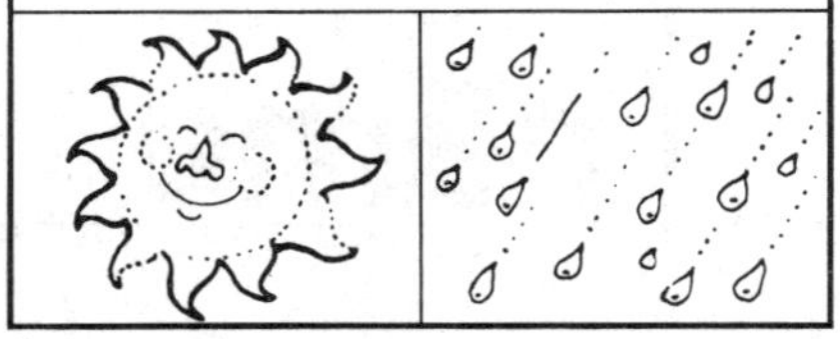

sad

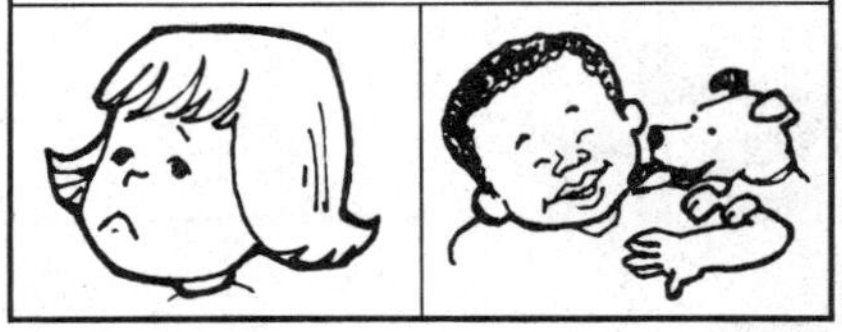

a mitt

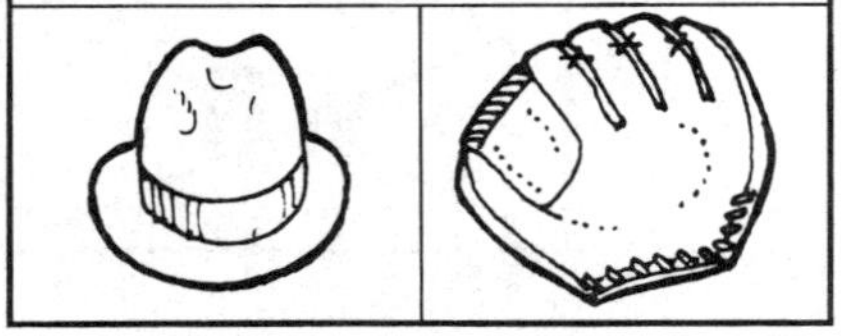

dish

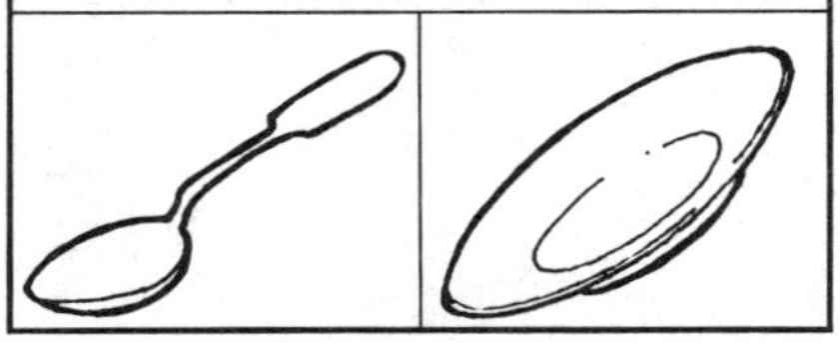

ēars

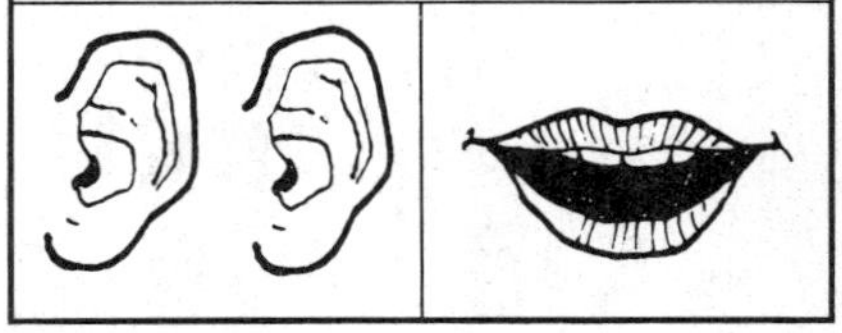

a cat

fan

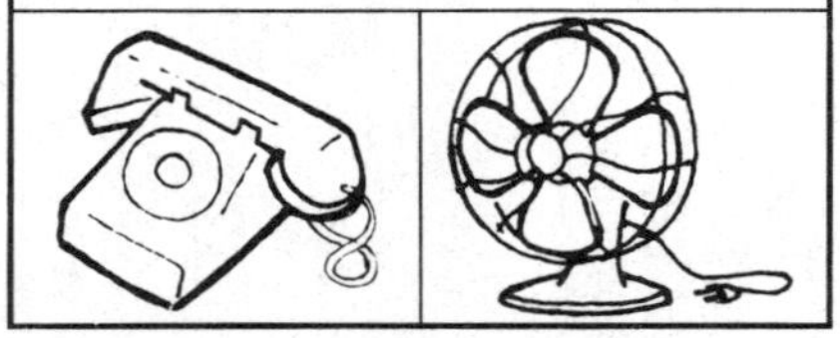

hē

NAME ______________________________

thē fish had fun.

thē fish had fun.

k k

c

o

d

t

had

mom

fun

ham

shē

~~this~~

this his thē this

littl_e this this will this

this not is mād_e

sēē this this shot this

a fish

fat

sit

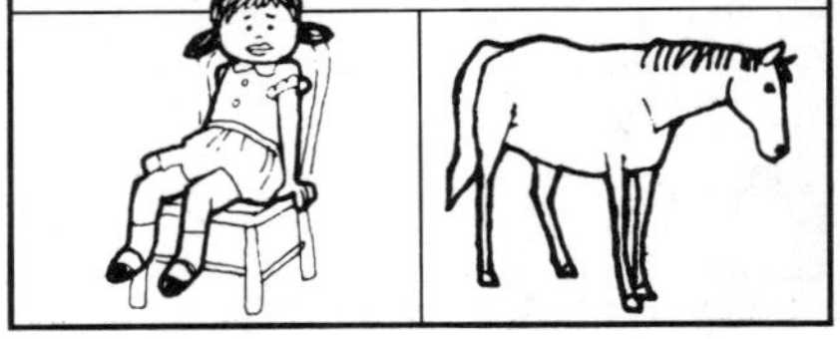

hill

fēēt

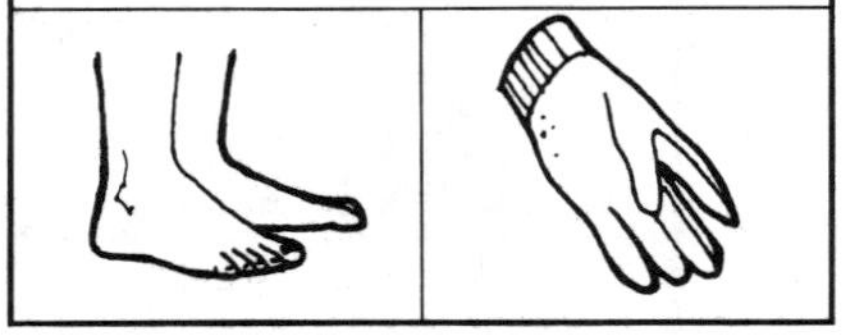

a rug

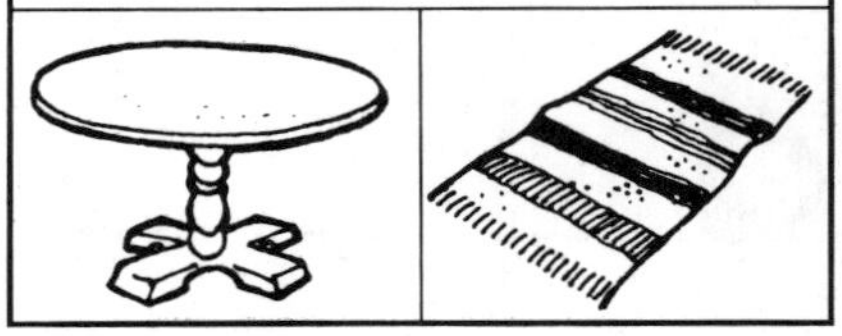

a man

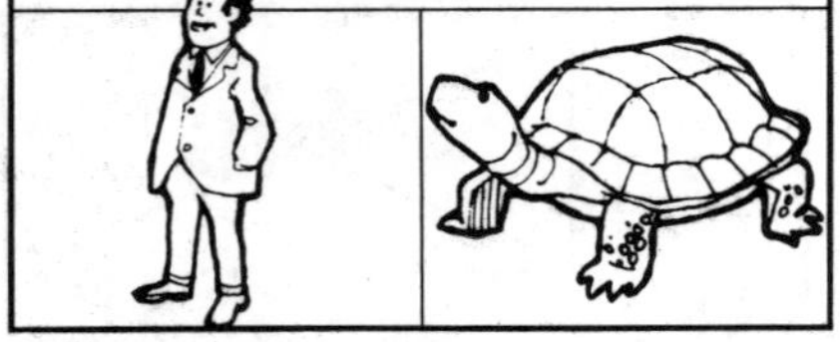

sand

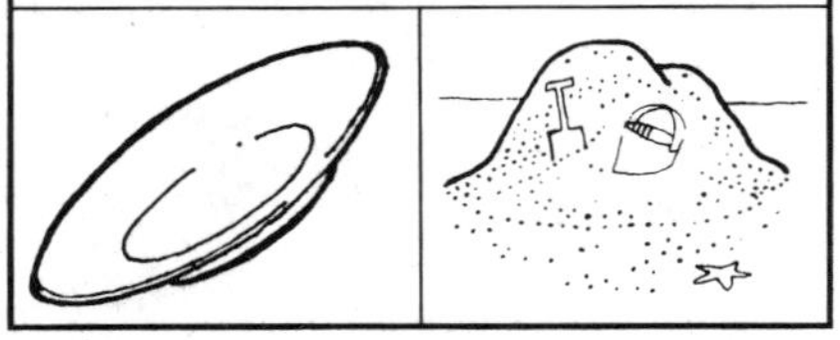

hut

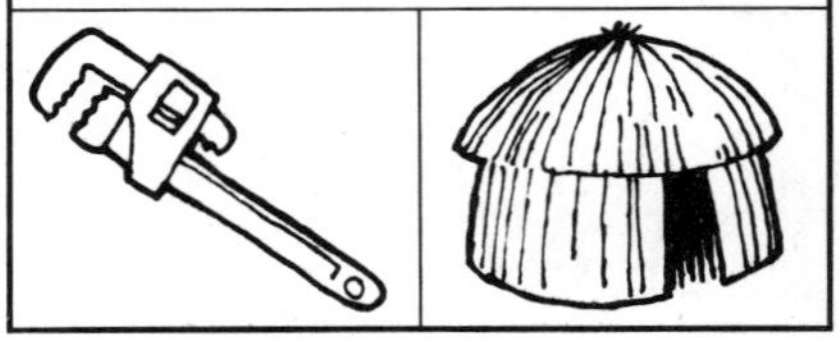

hat

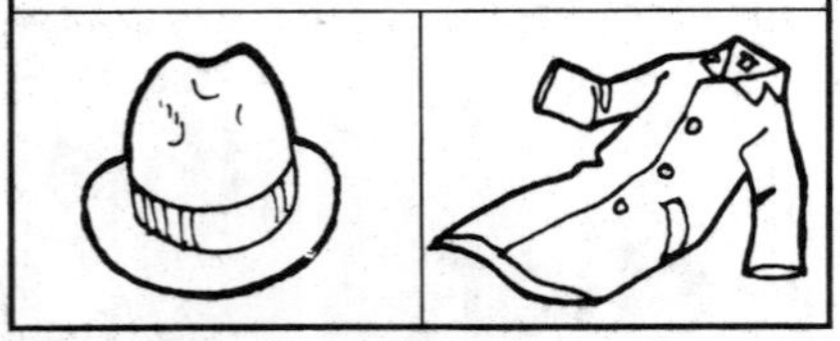

a dish

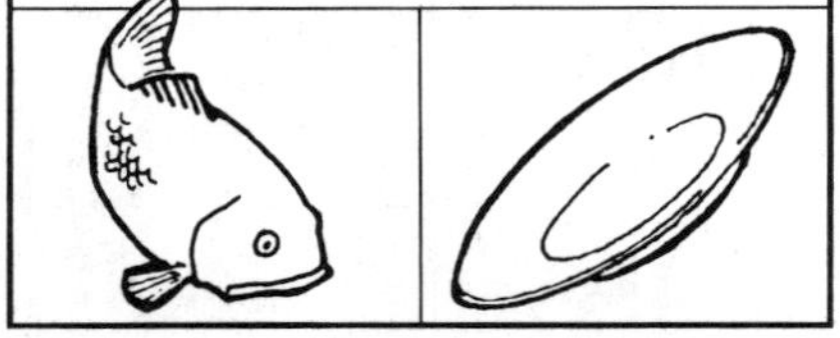

tāil

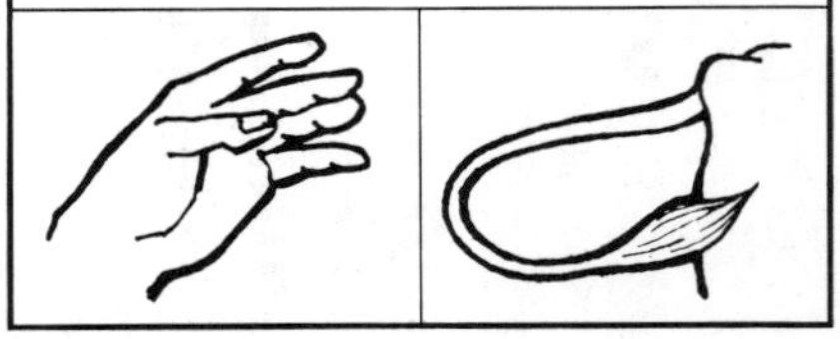

Printed in the United States of America.

shē sat on a hill.

shē sat on a hill.

o _ _ _ _

k k _ _

I _ _ _

ā _ _ _ _

h _ _ _ _

did

not

cat

fēēt

sick

is

is with is fun is did is

is this

wish is is

lāke is sand is is his thē

a dish

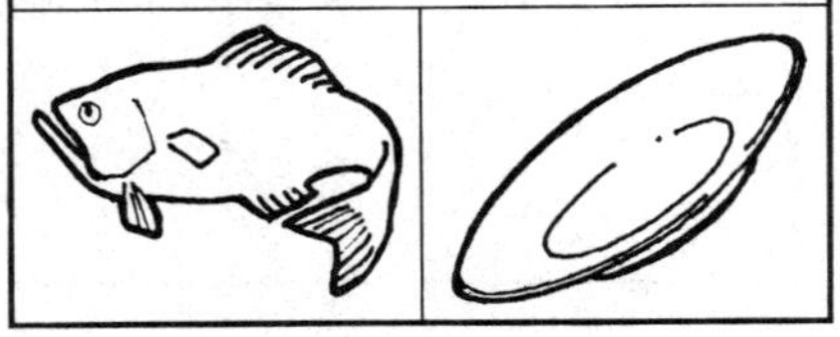

shē

rag

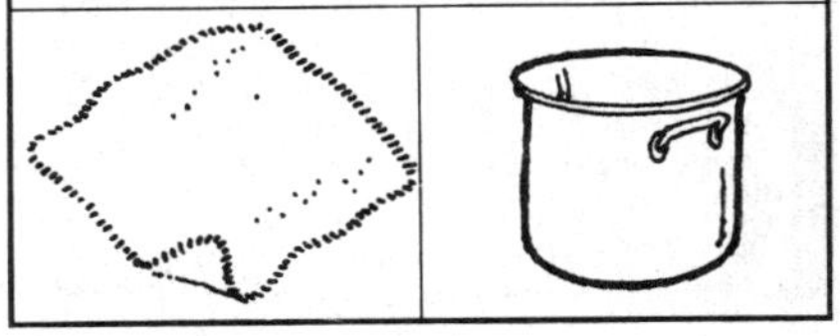

fēēt

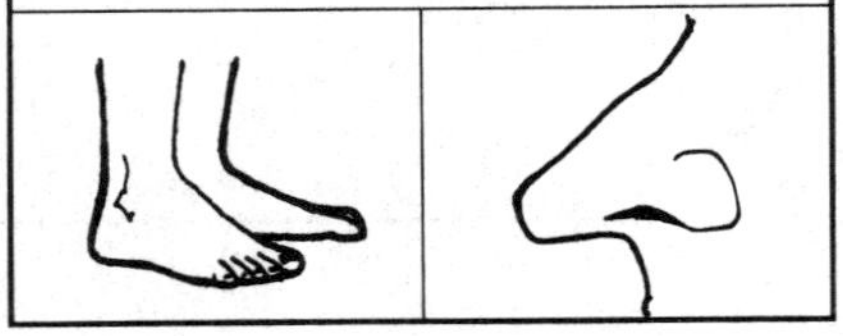

shack

a mitt

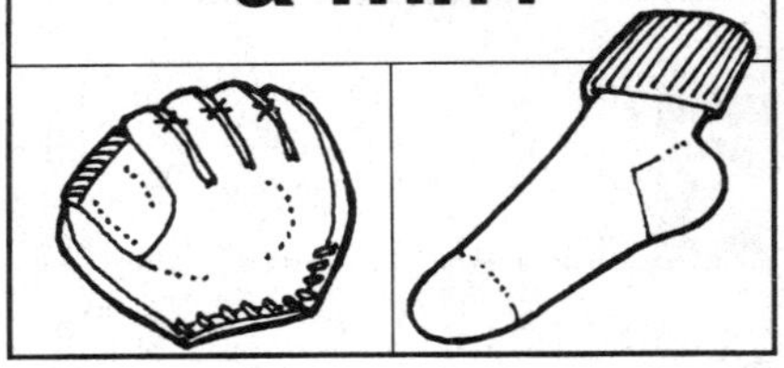

a rāke

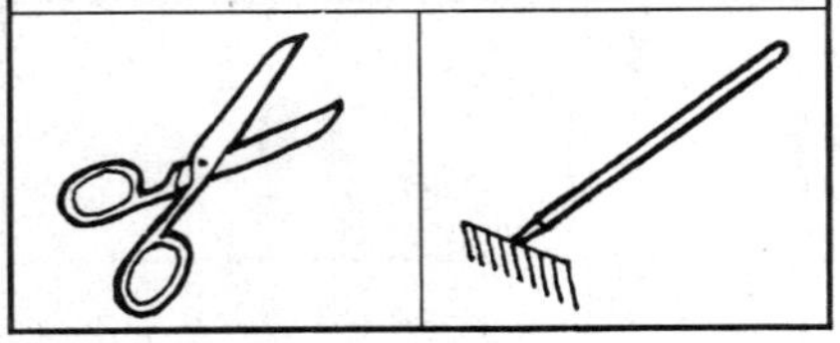

him

fan

ēars

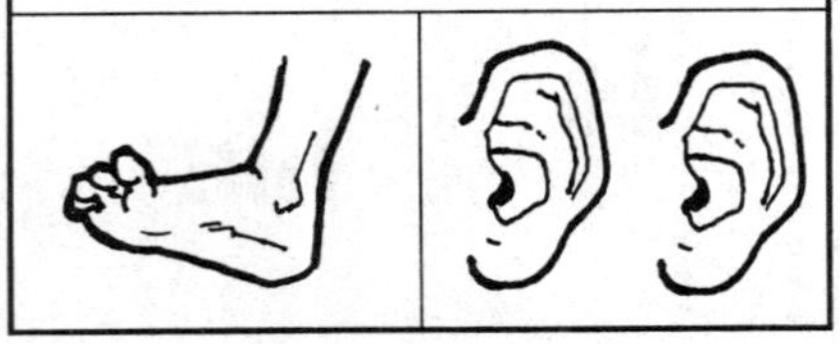

lāke

sit

Printed in the United States of America.

I am lāte. I āte ham on a hill.

I āte and āte. and now I am

lāte. I will run.

hē has a fat cat. hē has fun with his fat cat.

his mom has a little cat. shē has fun with thē little cat. thē little cat has fun in thē sand.

Printed in the United States of America.

shē said, "I āte."

shē said, "I āte."

n _ _ _ _	is
k k k _ _	his
c _ _ _ _	sēē
m _ _ _	hat
th _ _	sand

~~shē~~

shē said fēēt

shack shē

hē shē shē

little

shē

shē got shē

shē shē

cow shē thē tāil

rāke

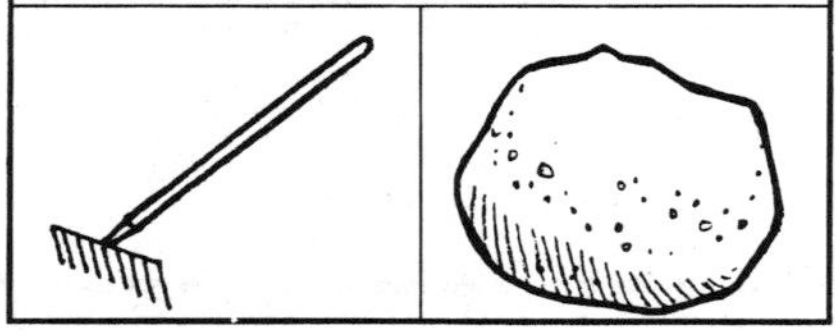

a dish

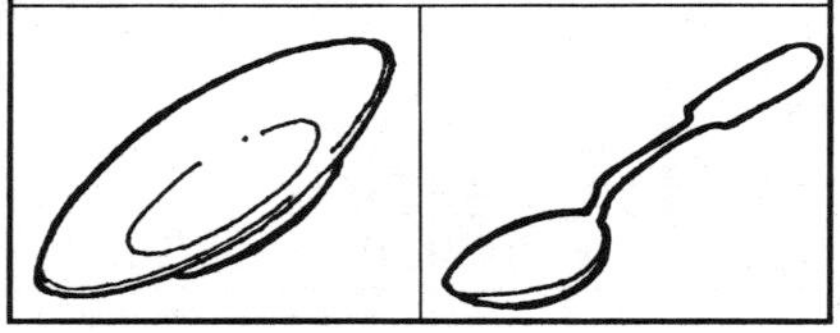

cat

mom

tāil

little

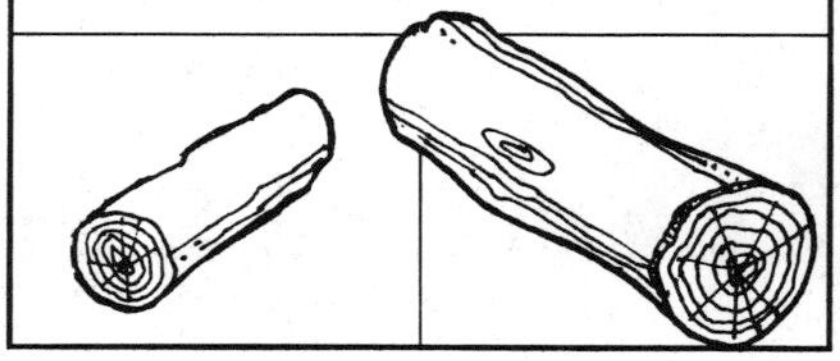

sand

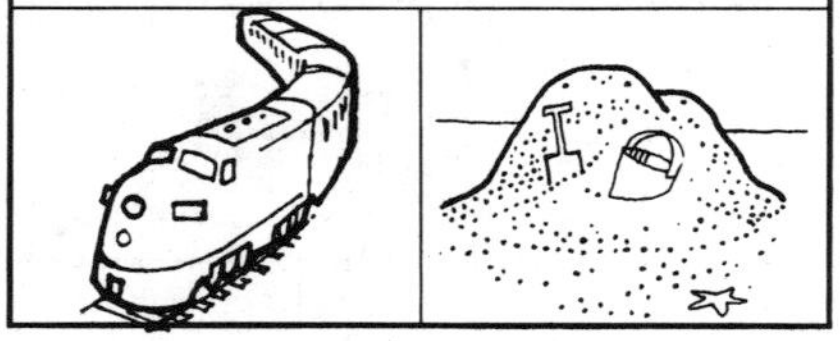

a rag

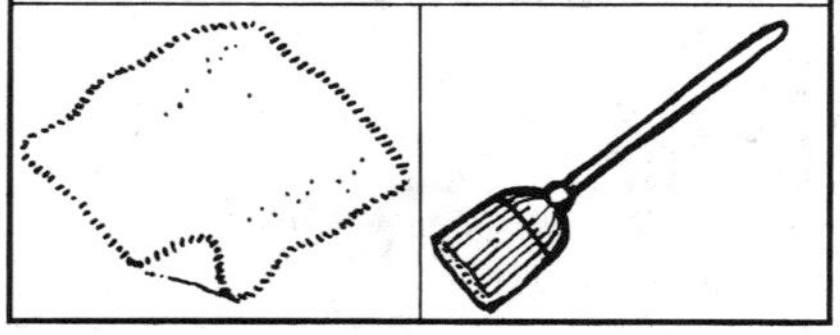

lāke

a hill

ēars

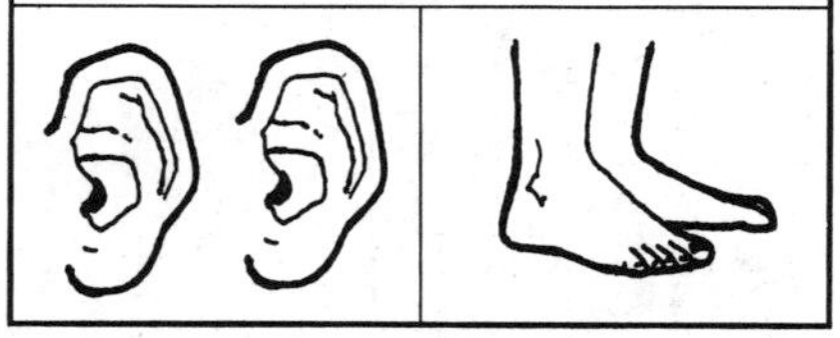

sack

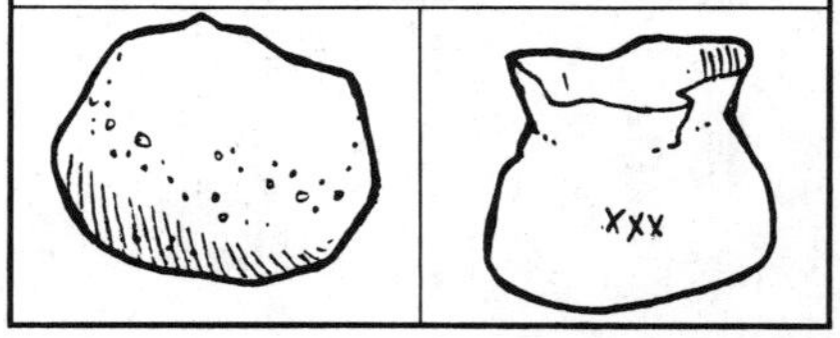

NAME ____________________

shē said, "I am mē."

shē said, "I am mē."

h _ _ _ _	rock
d _ _ _ _	māil
k _ _ _ _	fat
s _ _ _ _	fun
ē _ _ _ _	wē

that fish that āte that

hot that at that

that fat that

now

gun that mom this that

that

hill

hē

sad

a lock

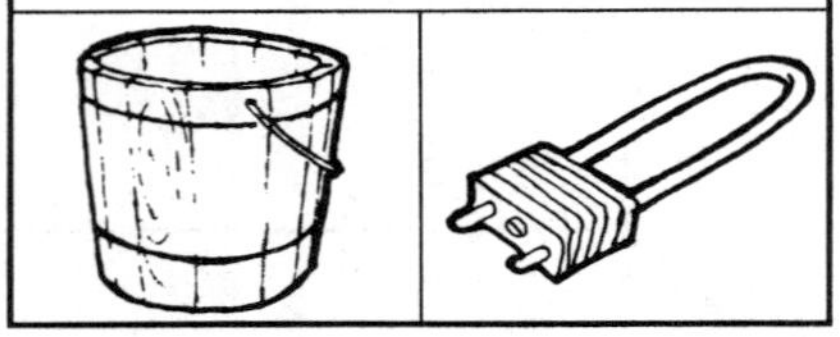

fat

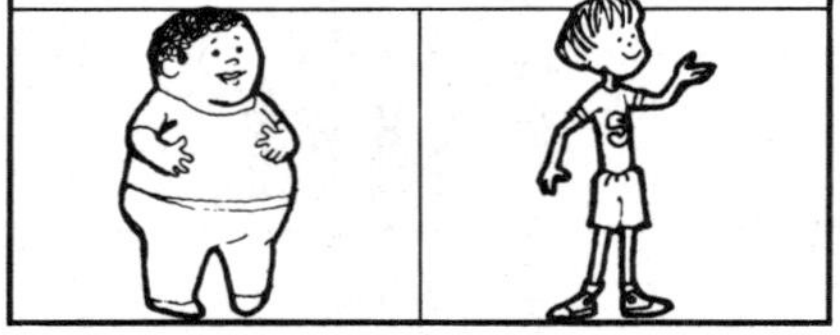

hut

a fish

mom

fēēt

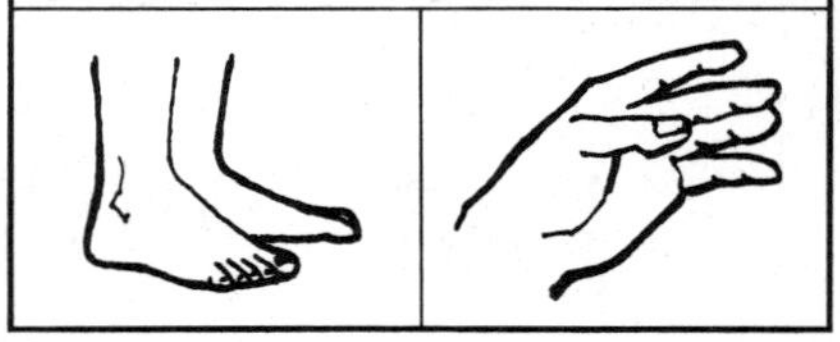

tāil

rāin

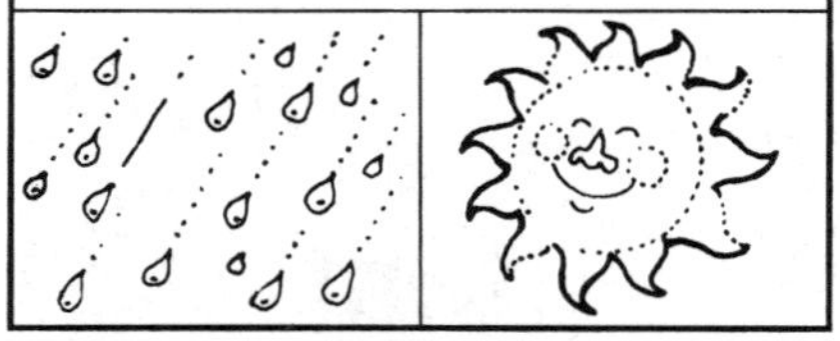

a fan

Printed in the United States of America.

NAME ____________________

shē was not mad.

shē was not mad.

f _ _ _ _

k _ _ _ _

c _ _ _ _

r _ _ _ _

m _ _ _

can

dish

āte

man

got

~~nō~~

nō gāte nō am not hat nō sand nō nō nō tāil nō nō wish nō hit cow nō

gāte

a cow

māil

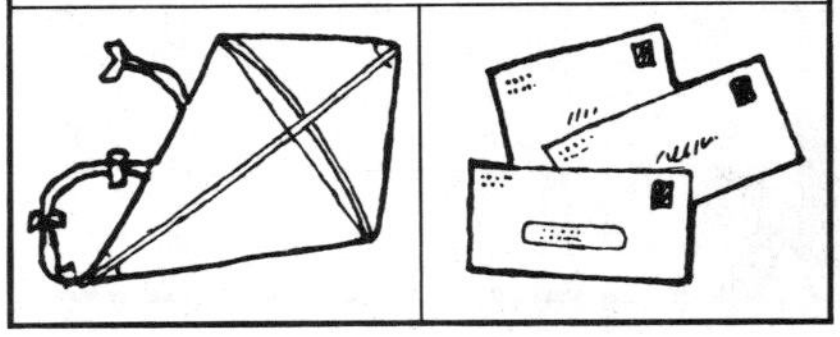

dish

sock

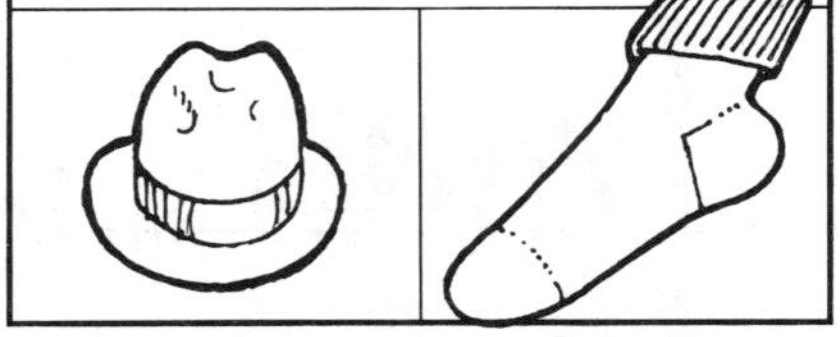

a cat

shē

a rāke

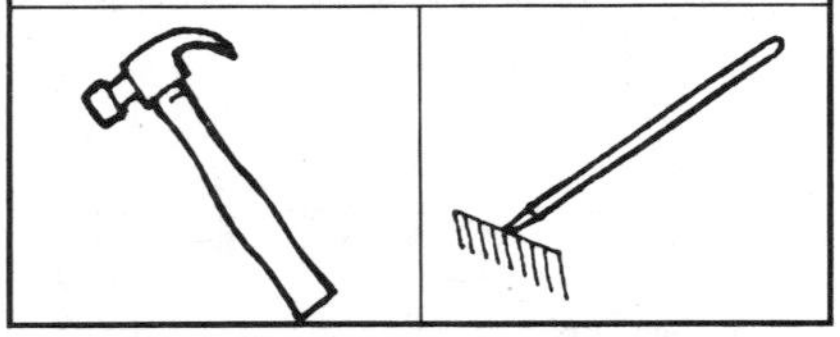

rāin

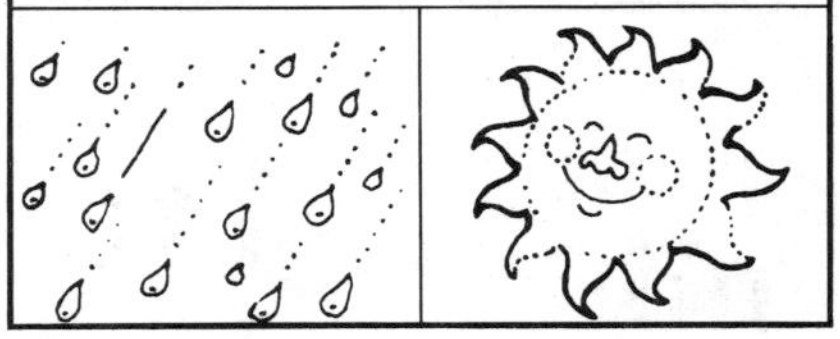

him

a shack

hill

Printed in the United States of America.

NAME ______________________

hē sat with a cat.

hē sat with a cat.

ō ō ō _ _	sat
k _ _ _ _	I
o _ _ _ _	mē
ā _ _ _ _	his
u _ _ _ _	fit

~~thē~~

thē shē cat thē

hē thē āte thē fish hug thē

thē nō thē little thē thē lick

a cow

fan

fish

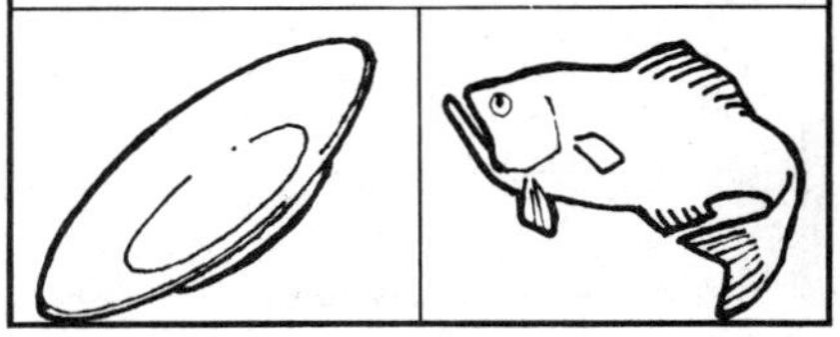

lāke

mom

sand

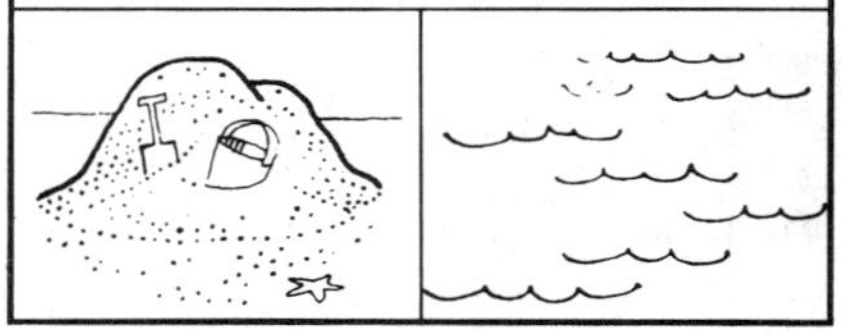

ēars

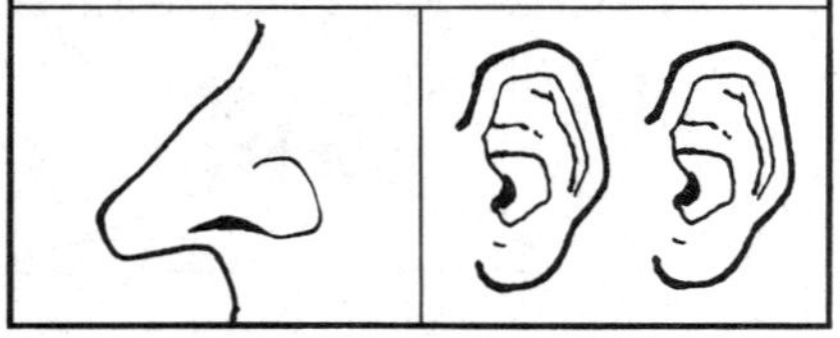

a mitt

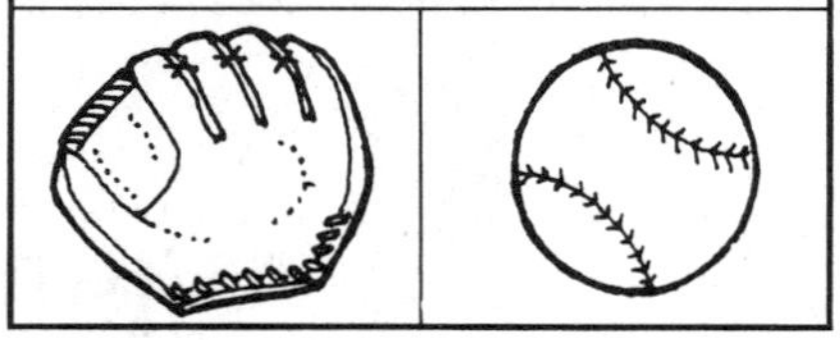

fēēt

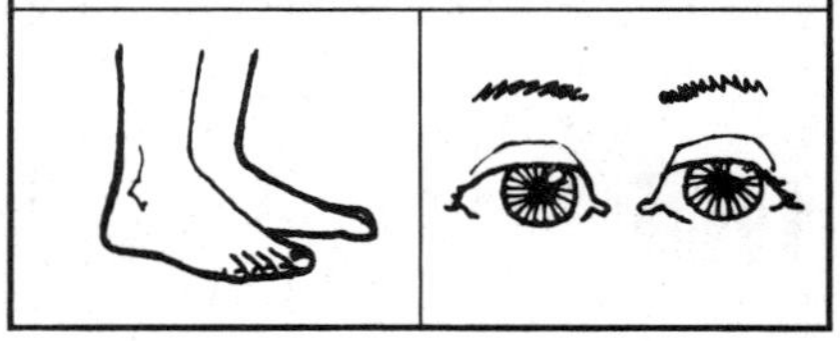

a rag

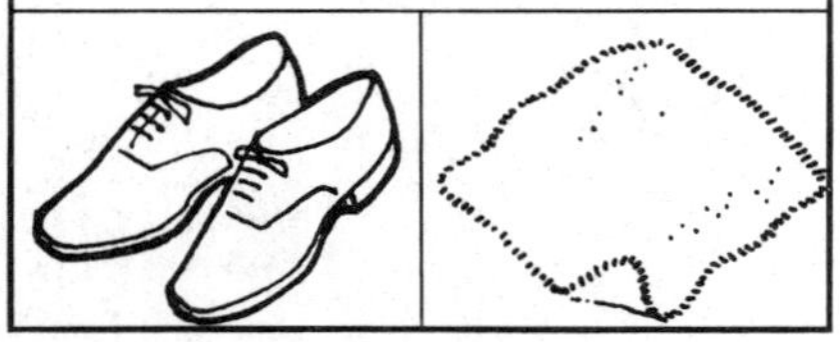

lock

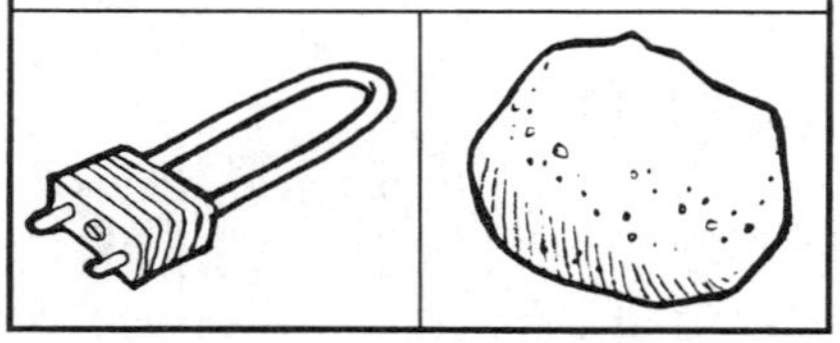

him

Printed in the United States of America.

NAME ______________________________

hē has nō tēēth.

hē has nō tēēth.

k _ _ _ _	kick
o o _ _ _	got
ō _ _ _ _	said
m _ _ _	cow
ē _ _ _ _	with

~~if~~

him

if

said

if

nō

if

kick

if

now

if

if

rug

thē

if

if

wish

if

fēēl

lāke

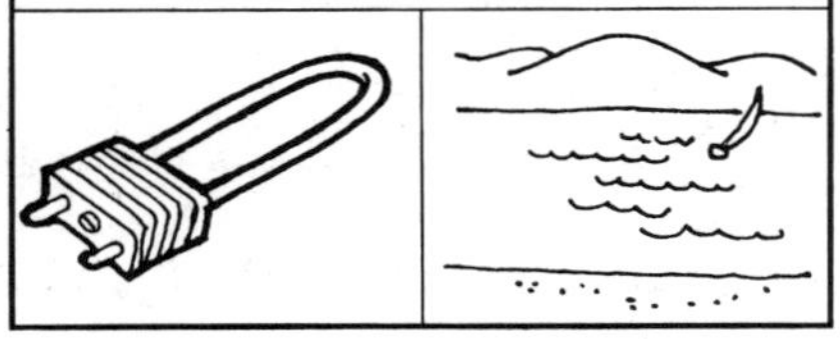

cow

tāil

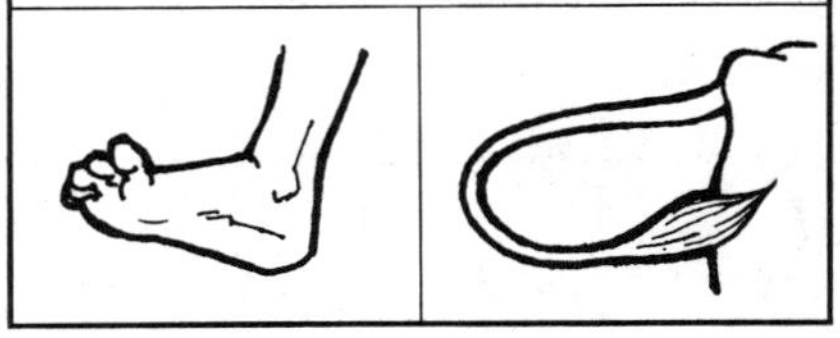

shē

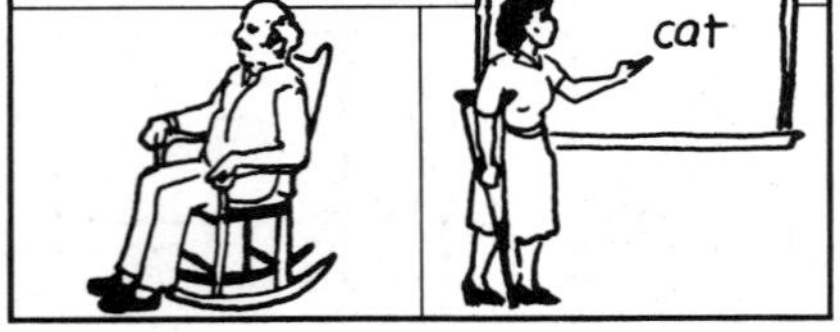

dish

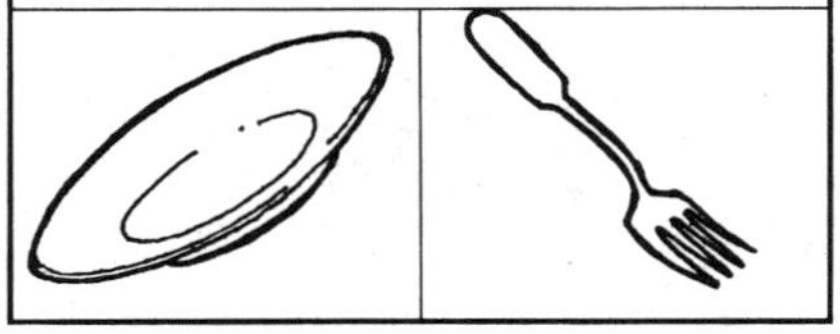

a rāke

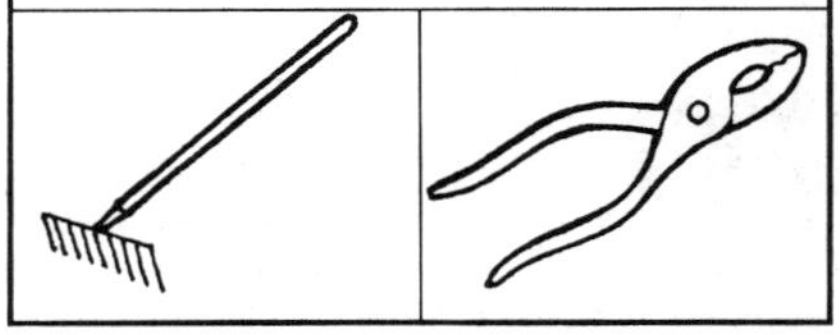

hill

a shack

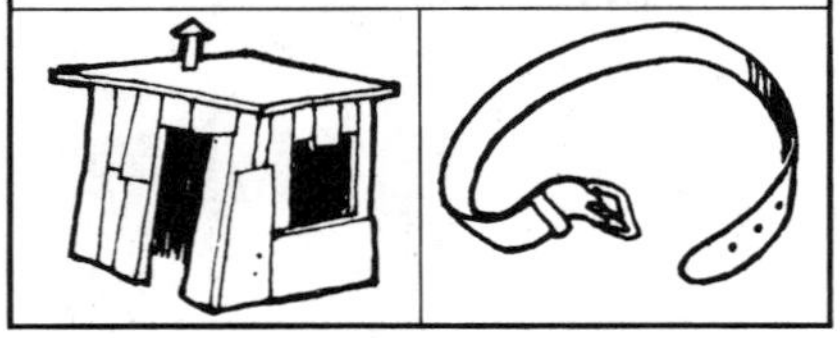

sick

a cat

sack

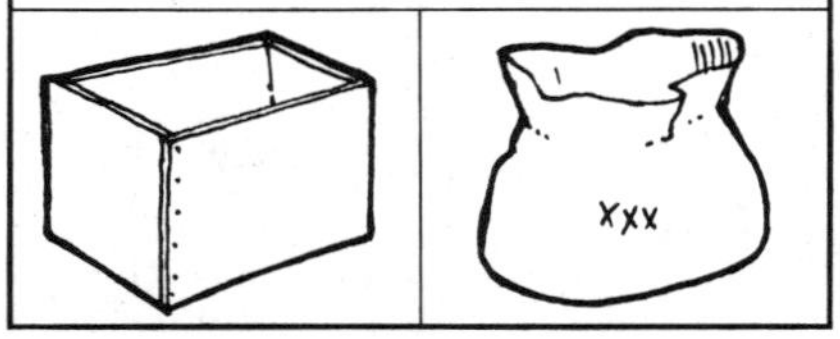

fat

Printed in the United States of America.

a fish āte a rock. thē fish said, "I āte a rock."

a cow āte thē fish. thē cow said, "I āte a fish. and now I fēēl sick."

shē was not mad at him. did

shē hit him? nō, nō, nō. did shē

hug him? nō, nō, nō. did shē

kiss him?

Printed in the United States of America.

NAME ____________________

I can kiss a cat.

I can kiss a cat.

ō ō ō _ _	lāke
d _ _ _ _	now
i _ _ _ _	wish
th _ _	lick
l _ _ _ _	sad

him him nō ~~him~~

hit him him if him

hug hat ēat

him cāke him him

him kiss will

a rug

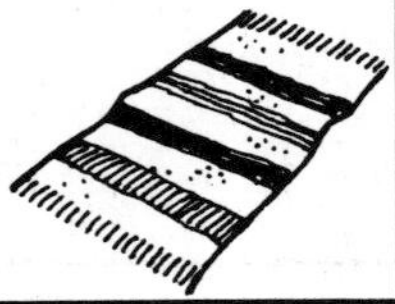

fēēt

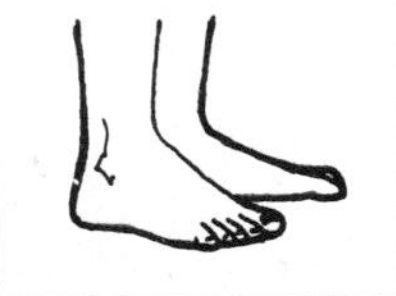

him

hut

māil

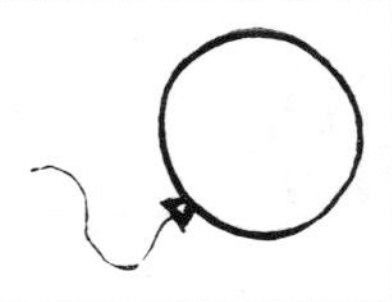

ēars

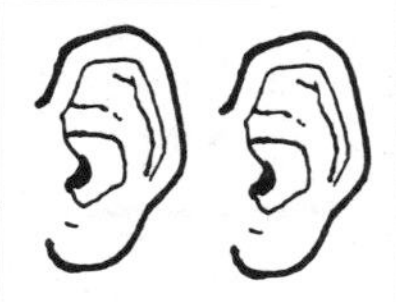
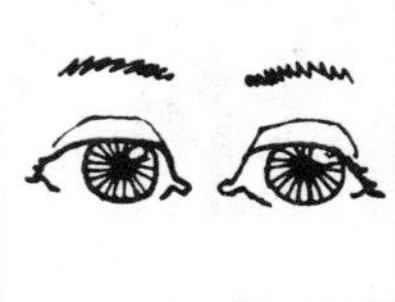

kiss

mom

a lāke

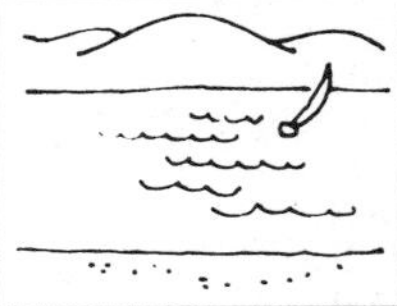

a rock

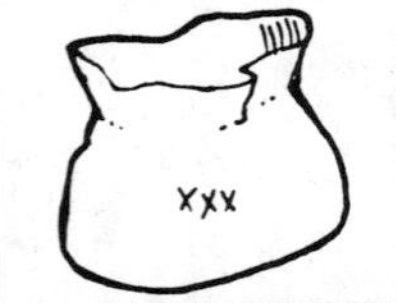

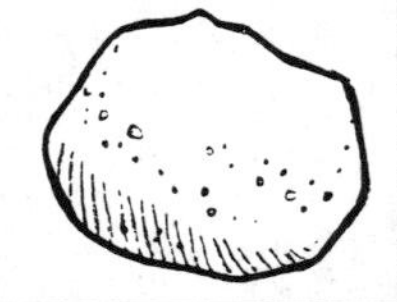

hat

lick

Printed in the United States of America.

a cat is on thē cow.

a cat is on thē cow.

ō _ _ _ _	sō
k _ _ _ _	run
I _ _ _	mad
sh _ _	nō
u _ _ _ _	sick

~~and~~

thē and lick

and sat rat nō and

and man

and and and

āte

sand and him and

a cat

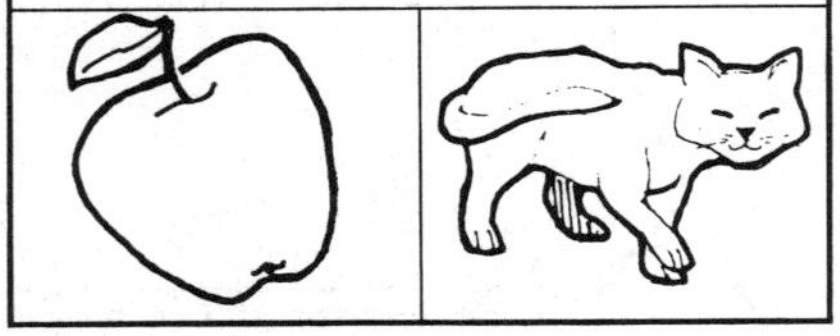

sand

shē

sad

a fish

shack

a rāke

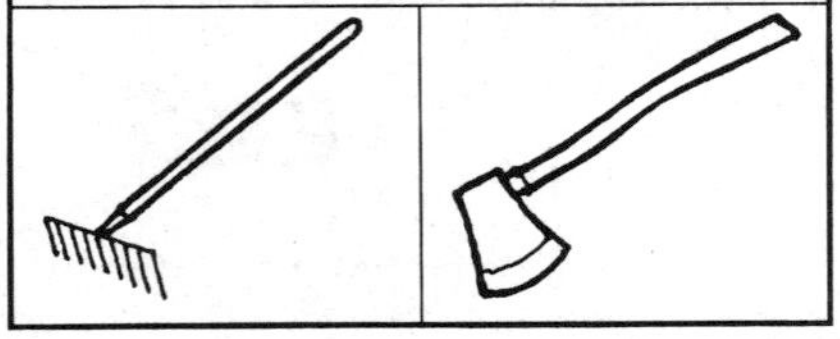

sit

a cow

lock

hē

mitt

Printed in the United States of America.

NAME ______________________

I can hōld thē hats.

I can hōld thē hats.

ā _ _ _ _	cāke
ō _ _ _ _	fan
o _ _ _ _	it
a _ _ _ _	was
v v _ _	man

~~cow~~

cow have cow cow kiss cat if cow wish cow cow cow cow now how lāte cow fēēt

nōse

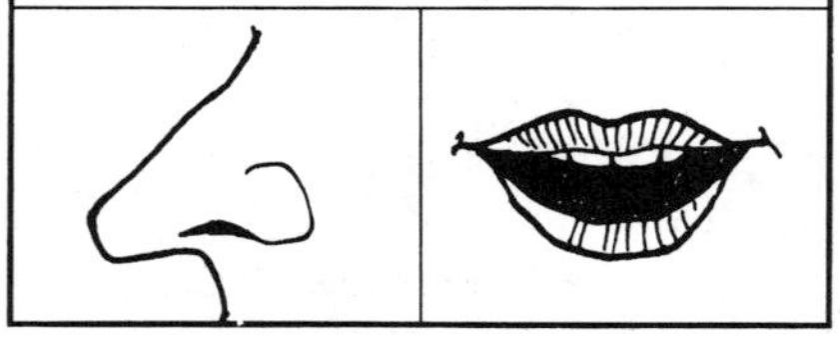

a cat

fat

rag

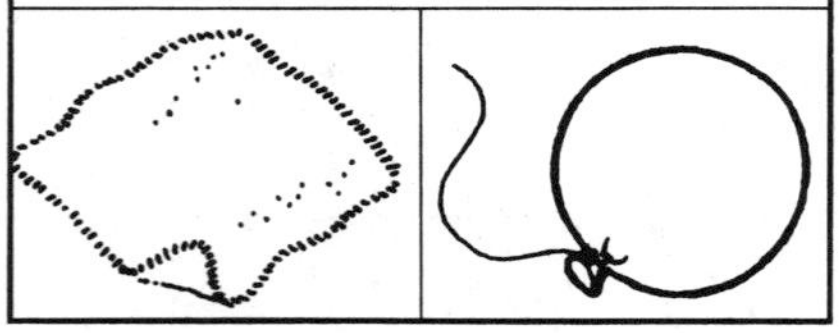

mom

a dish

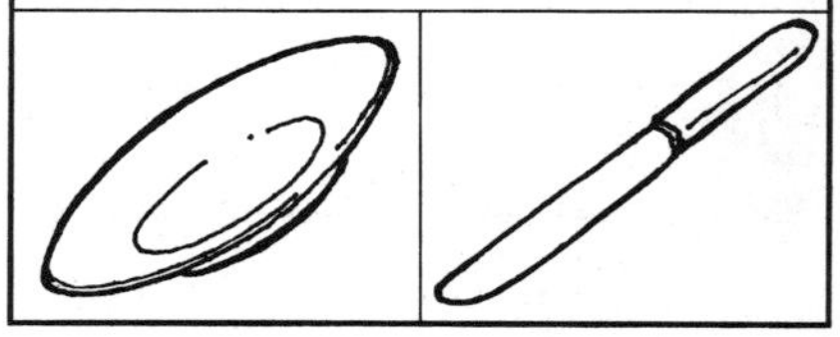

lāke

fēēt

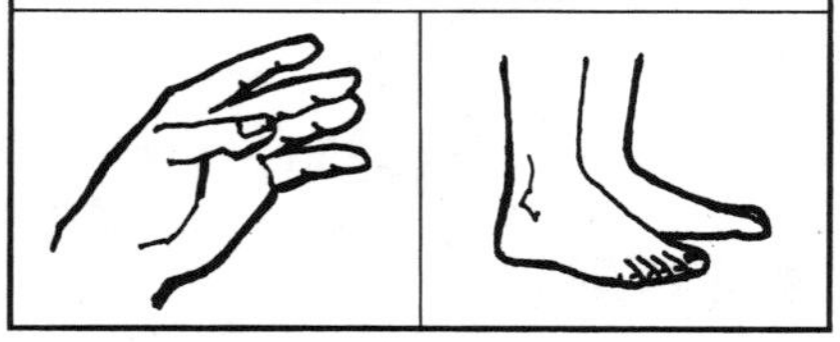

tēēth

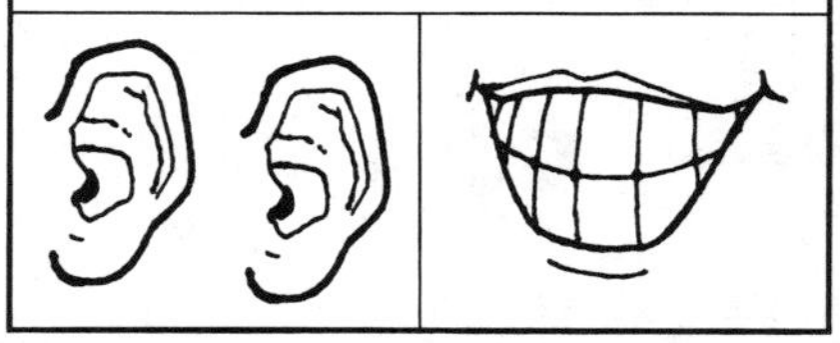

kiss

a cow

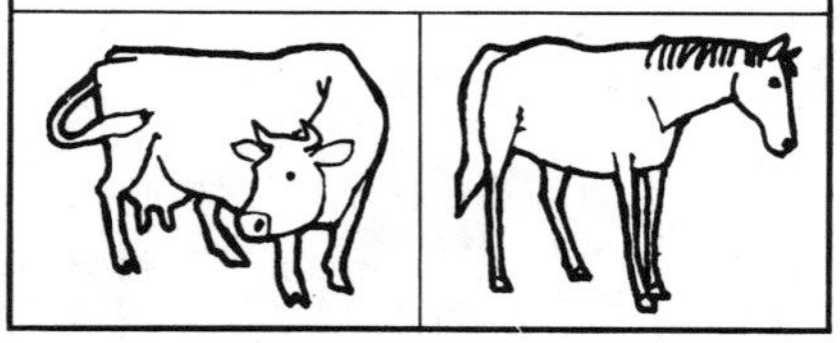

lick

Printed in the United States of America.

NAME ______________________

wē have sacks.

wē have sacks.

th ___ ___	rag
sh ___ ___	him
h ___ ___ ___ ___	thē
l ___ ___ ___ ___	rug
g ___ ___ ___ ___	sēē

~~can~~

can can nō can
fish can
cat teeth
can can
sand and
can
cow can
can is not

kitten

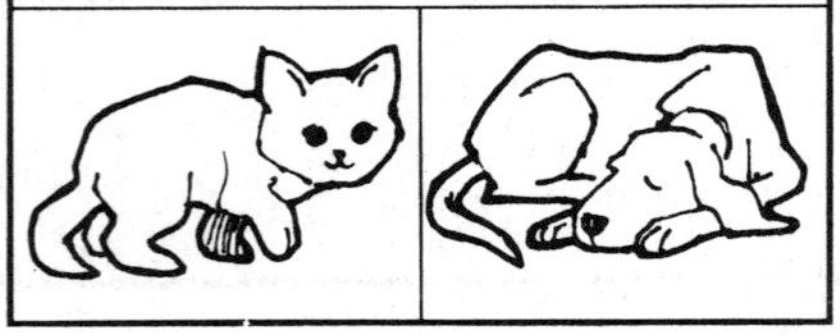

hit

ēars

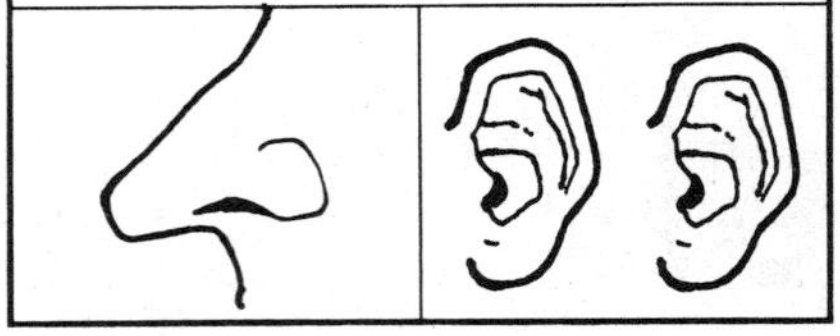

shē

a sack

sand

rāke

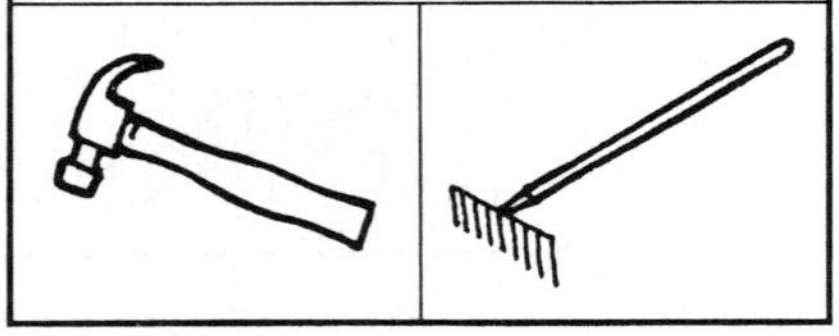

a rock

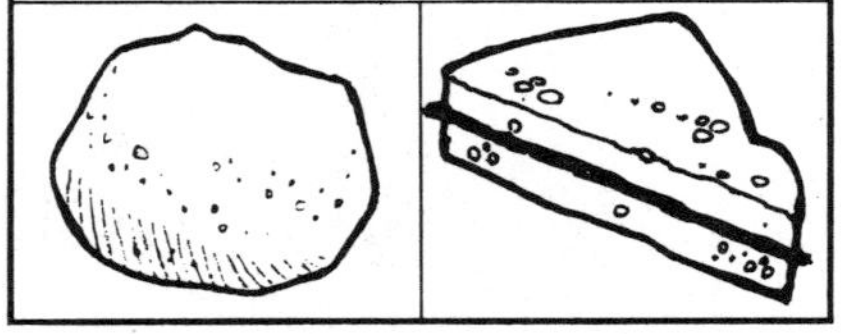

lock

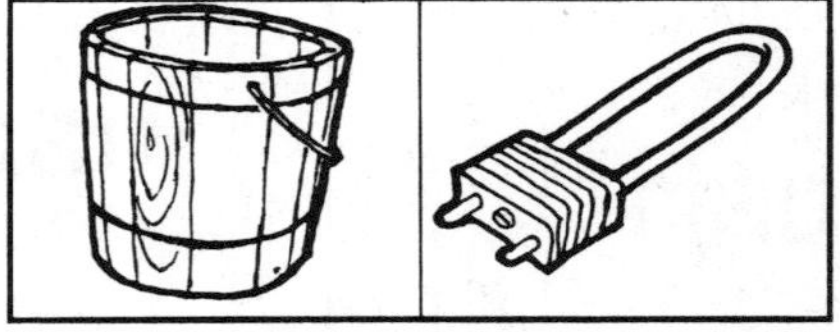

a rug

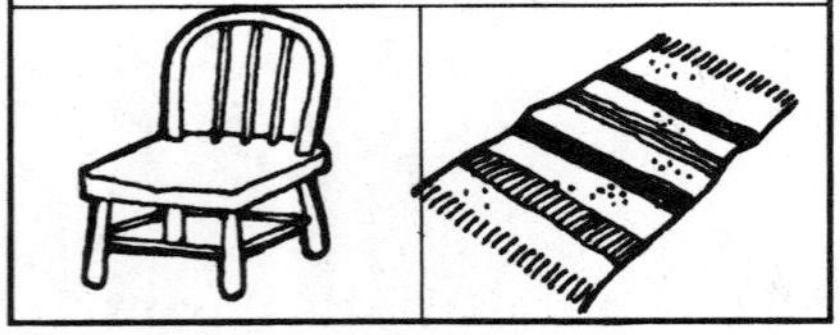

tēēth

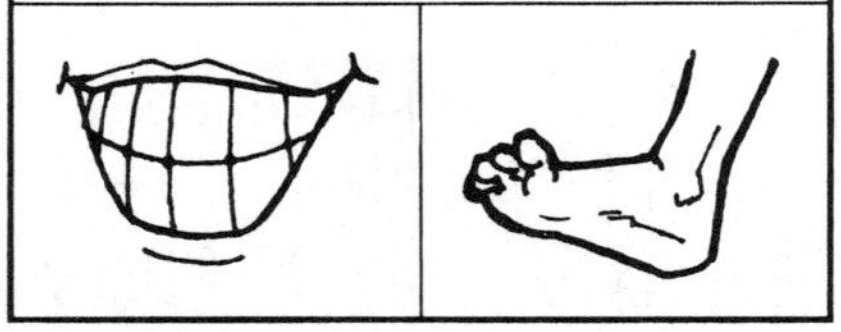

fan

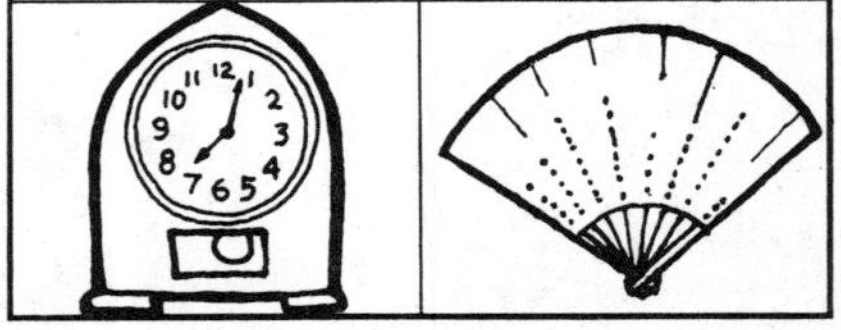

Printed in the United States of America.

NAME ______________________

thē ōld man shāves.

thē ōld man shāves.

v v ___ ___	in
w ___ ___ ___	can
n ___ ___ ___ ___	gāte
u ___ ___ ___ ___	this
h ___ ___ ___ ___	a

~~now~~

now lick now

not now mē

now now now if

āte

kitten cow now

now

can has now

a cow

lāke

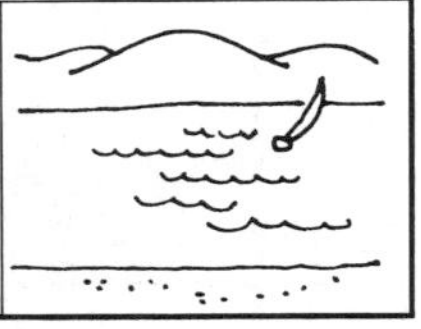

hill

mom

kiss

a rock

tēēth

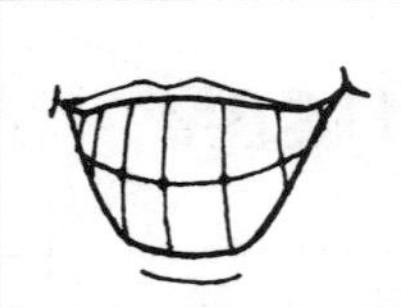

mitt

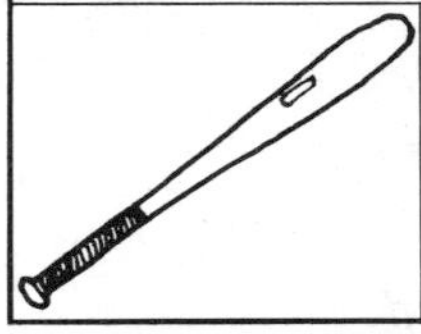

a dish

a fish

nōse

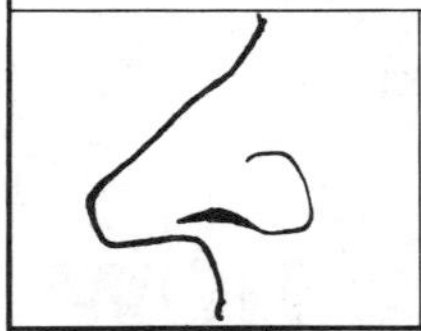
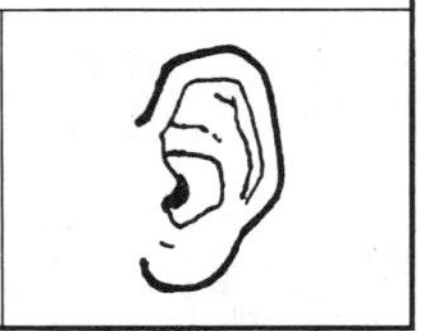

shack

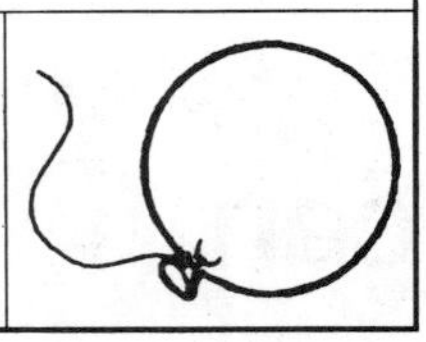

Printed in the United States of America.

I can kiss a cat. I can kiss

a kitten.

can a cow kiss mē? nō. a cow

can not kiss mē. a cow can

lick mē.

can a cat lick a kitten?

wē have hats. I can hōld thē

hats. thē cow can hōld thē hats.

an ōld man can hōld thē hats.

can a fat rat hōld thē hats?

Printed in the United States of America.

NAME ____________________

give mē a sock.

give mē a sock.

ō	lāte
I	that
v v	hōld
k	rock
u	mē

~~hats~~

hats sit hats at hats

rock littl hats ōld hats hats

now have hats can wē hats hats

thē hats

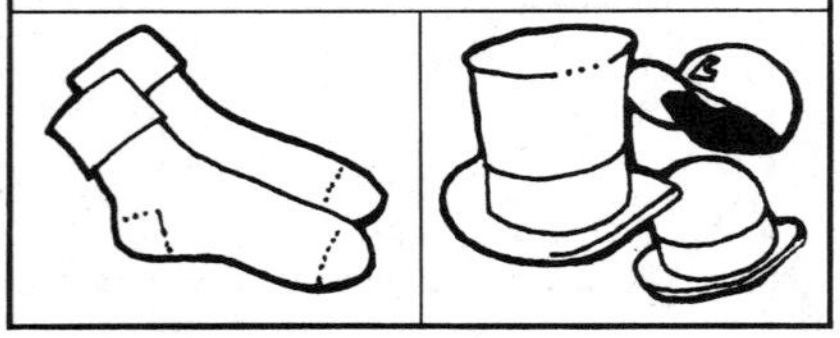

ōld

a sack

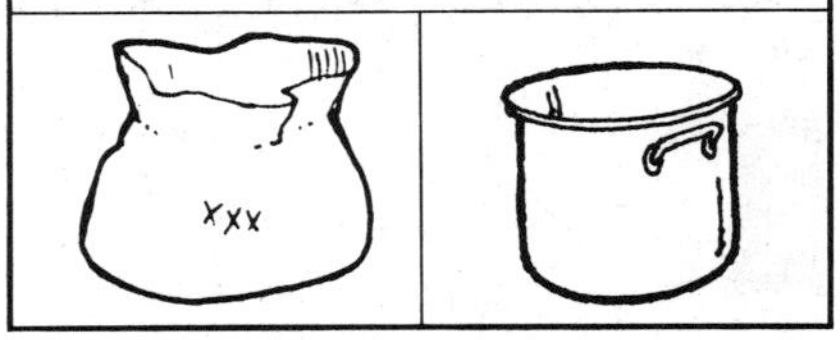

mad

ēars

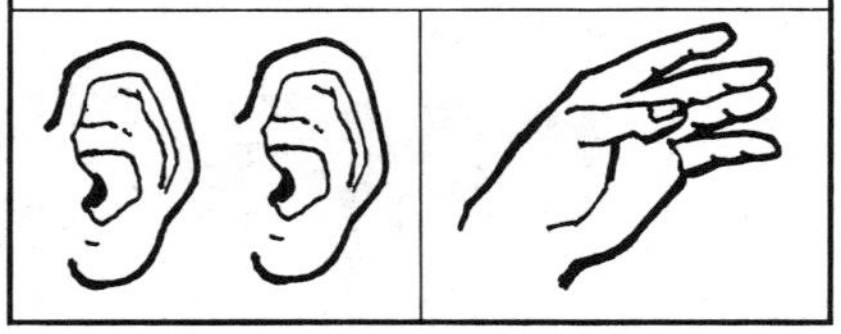

mom

a dish

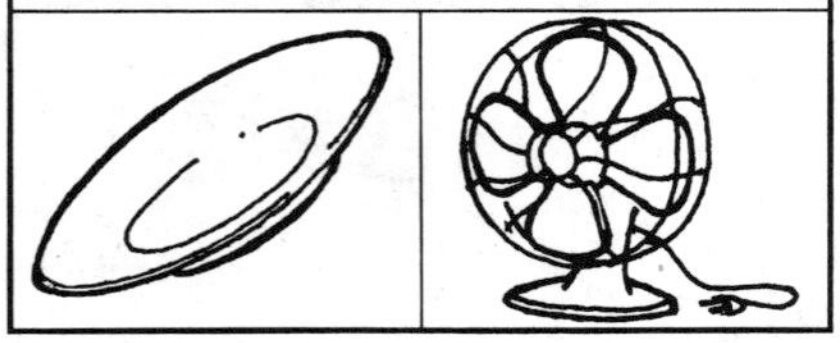

nōse

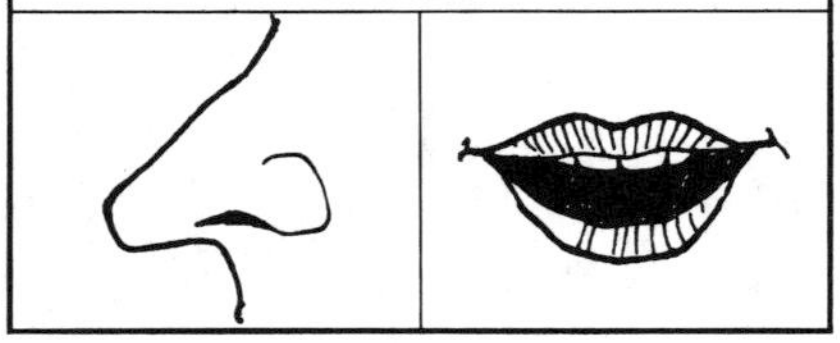

lock

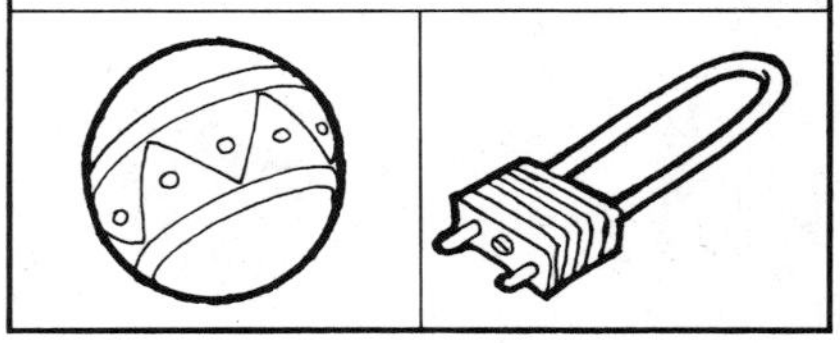

fēēt

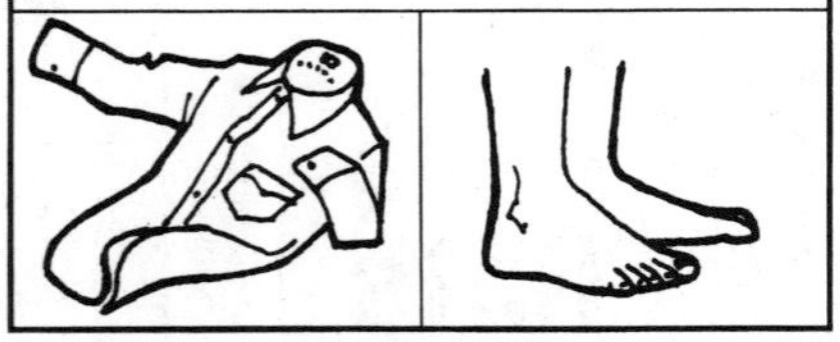

sad

kitten

Printed in the United States of America.

NAME

thē man was cōld.

thē man was cōld.

w	shē
k	mitt
v	ran
f	hats
ā	said

~~nēēd~~

will nēēd did nēēd

nēēd can fēēt

nō nēēd

sand nēēd nēēd

tēēth

nēēd nēēd

hōld ēat

nēēd

a sack

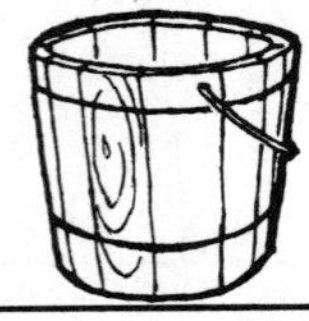 

tēēth

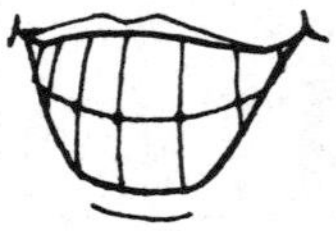 

thē rocks

 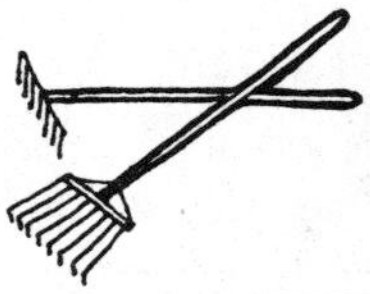

kiss

shē

shack

 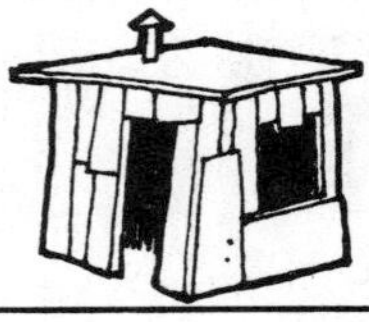

fan

a man

sand

a tāil

dish

sit

Printed in the United States of America.